THE "HOW TO" OF
CHRISTIANITY

Derek Stringer

Acknowledgements

I wish to express my grateful thanks to David and Pat Holme for their proof-reading and helpful comments. If there are mistakes in this book, that is my responsibility.

I have used several sources in preparing this book and I happily acknowledge those known to me. They include:

The Saving Life of Christ by Major W. Ian Thomas, D.S.O., T.D. This is a classic book that has helped countless believers understand the 'how to' of Christianity. My copy is published by Torchbearer Publications, Capernwray Hall, Carnforth, Lancashire. LA6 1AG. United Kingdom.

Pastor David Dykes.Texas.

Pastor Mike Andrus, First Evangelical Free Church, Wichita.

God bless you both in your ministries.

DEDICATION

To my wife, Pauline, whose encouragement and support make my ministry possible and who models the principles of this book and to my daughters Tracy and Clare and my son-in-law Tony. I am blessed through my wonderful family.

To my friend David Leigh, who has prayed regularly for me through the years and keeps me from becoming a heretic!

To Chalmers Dobson, who is both a brother in Christ and a colleague at Good News Broadcasting. I thank him for his support and his administrative skills that enable me to concentrate on teaching God's Word.

Contents

Chapter 1

How To Crack The Great Mystery

Most people love a good mystery. That is why Agatha Christie has had such a long running play in the West End of London and years after her death, her books and TV dramas are appreciated. Many people enjoy crosswords and Sudoku and try to solve mysteries and puzzles. Let me give you an example of one mystery and see if you can solve it before you read on.

The Mystery: A carrot, a scarf and five buttons were found in a field. If nobody placed them on the grass, how did they get there? The Solution: They are the remains of a snowman after a thaw.

For many mysteries, finding out the answer takes away the interest or importance of the whole thing. That is certainly not true of the mystery that I am referring to because it is history's most important mystery. Let me give you some general background information about mysteries in the Bible:

- The word "mystery" is found twenty-seven times in the New Testament.
- In the Bible, a "mystery" does not refer to something that is permanently hidden.
- A "mystery" is a particular truth that God keeps secret for a period of time.
- When God decides the time is right, He fully reveals what that particular truth is.

Before we read the Scriptures and I write about the Bible's greatest mystery, I want to start by giving you three clues to see if you can figure it out for yourself:

Clue One: It can make you rejoice even when you suffer
Clue Two: It was hidden for many ages
Clue Three: It can make you a complete person.

Clue One: It can make you rejoice even when you suffer because the power behind this mystery is so great. You can smile even in the most painful times of life.

Before he was converted to Christ, Paul was a fanatical religious terrorist. He worked as a self-proclaimed hit man in Jerusalem arresting Christians, imprisoning them and giving his approval to their execution. There is an irony in Paul's story. After he became a Christian, he spent a lot of time in jail and suffered more than most of us would want to read about or imagine. By Paul's own admission in Second Corinthians, he had been:

- Beaten eight times.
- Shipwrecked three times.
- Stoned so badly he was left for dead.

But rather than complain about his suffering, Paul boasted and rejoiced about them. Why? He had found the answer to a mystery that enabled him to deal with pain and adversity with a positive attitude.

There is a beautiful painting by Baron Von Lind depicting Paul in prison as an old, emaciated man. But rather than resigning himself to bitterness or simply giving up to his fate, he is seen praying. There are scraps of papyrus seen at his side representing his ministry of sending letters to believers to encourage and teach them. Instead of complaining about what he was suffering, Paul wrote in Colossians:

"Now I rejoice in what was suffered for you." Colossians 1:24

He wanted to be free to preach and start new churches but he had discovered the answer to a mystery that allowed him to see beyond the prison bars. While he was in prison, waiting to be executed, he sent letters to Philemon, his friend and helper and to the Christians at Ephesus, Philippi and Colossae.

Have you experienced this power that enables you to thrive during the tough times of life and not just to survive them? That is the first clue.

Clue Two: It was hidden for many ages because this mystery has not always been known. Paul writes that although it has been hidden for generations, it is now disclosed. This mystery was not revealed to the people who lived in Old Testament times, no matter who they were. So, although we can know this mystery:

- Moses never understood it.
- Elijah was clueless about it.
- David who was described by the Prophet Samuel as "a man after God's own heart" never knew about it.

The Old Testament refers to God's promises that He will save and deliver His people. But you never read how God intended to do it. That part was hidden. It was a mystery. Let us consider some well known verses.

I love the promise given in Isaiah 40:

"Those who hope in the Lord will renew their strength. They will soar on wings like eagles; they will run and not grow weary, they will walk and not be faint." Isaiah 40:31

That verse is an absolute promise of God. But how does God actually strengthen His children? Isaiah could not have answered that question. It was a mystery.

David wrote that wonderful promise in Psalm 23:

"Surely goodness and mercy shall follow me all the days of my life..." Psalm 23:6

What David wrote is true but David would have been stumped if you had said to him, "Please tell me how God makes that possible?" David might have stabbed at an answer but he could not give you the correct answer because at that time it was a mystery. But now we can know how God does these wonderful things. Only one more clue remains.

Clue Three: This mystery can make you a complete person. Paul tells us the reason why it was revealed. It was so that we could be presented perfect in Christ.

The word perfect used by Paul does not mean without flaw. It means "whole" or "complete." Let me give you some background information. During Old Testament times, the Jews lived under the Law of Moses. The only way to be a complete person then was to keep the Law. The Jews had to have a performance mentality because righteousness was established by how good or how bad they behaved. This mystery offers not only a new but a totally different standard.

I must write a word of caution about what still happens today. Sadly, some churches preach a performance standard based religion. In error they:

- Adopt and teach the obsolete Old Testament performance standard of the Law of Moses.
- Preach that salvation is a matter of conduct.
- Have their:
  - "Thou shalts"- A long list of "do's."
  - "Thou shalt nots"- A long list of "do nots."

Those who try to live under a performance based religion punish themselves in the process. Their motto for failure is: Try harder! But, trying to achieve an impossible standard of perfection is itself a formula for certain failure.

Let me make this quite plain. This mystery:

- Completely contradicts any performance standard based religion.
- Opposes the preaching of performance standards as a means of salvation.
- Is the only way that you can be a complete person.

Have you figured out the mystery from my three clues? We read about it in Paul's letter to the Colossians. Think about my clues as you read these words:

"Now I rejoice in what was suffered for you, and I fill up in my flesh what is still lacking in regard to Christ's afflictions, for the sake of his body, which is the church. I have become its servant by the commission God gave me to present to you the word of God in its fullness - the MYSTERY that has been kept hidden for ages and generations, but is now disclosed to the saints. To them God has chosen to make known among the Gentiles the glorious riches of this mystery, which is CHRIST IN YOU, the hope of glory. We proclaim him, admonishing and teaching everyone with all wisdom, so that we may present everyone perfect in Christ. To this end I labour, struggling with all his energy, which so powerfully works in me." Colossians 1:24-29

CHRIST IN YOU is history's greatest mystery. It is as profoundly simple as it is simply profound.

Christ in you:

- Enables you to remain positive during suffering.
- Is the way God fulfils all His precious promises.
- It is the HOW that was hidden for many centuries.
- Enables us to be complete persons.

True community is realised when the Christ in you connects with the Christ in me. The word "you" that Paul uses in these verses is plural. It is like a wonderful picture that is made up of hundreds of tiny photos of individuals and groups who make up the body of Christ. When we see the picture up close, it looks like a jumbled mess. But when we back away from it and gain a better perspective we can see the face of Jesus.

Christ in you does not mean that you have your own little personal divine essence like the New Agers teach. It is CHRIST IN YOU and CHRIST IN ME which makes CHRIST IN US. That is the church.

The New Testament teaches the dual truths of how we are "in Christ" and Christ is "in us." I first discovered the power of this profound mystery from reading books like The Saving Life of Christ by Major Ian Thomas. He wrote:

"To be in Christ—that makes you fit for heaven; but for Christ to be in you—that makes you fit for earth!

To be in Christ—that changes your destination; but for Christ to be in you—that changes your destiny!

To be in Christ—that makes heaven your home; but for Christ to be in you makes this world God's workshop."

That is the mystery and once you grasp it, it changes the way you understand your Christian life. I want to consider three personal applications of this mystery. They concern our:

- Salvation
- Security
- Strength

The First Personal Application: Salvation

Do not misunderstand what Salvation is:

- It is not religion
- It is Jesus living in you!

Jesus shocked the religious leaders by saying that the Kingdom of God is inside the body. He was not talking about some kind of divine spark or other new age mumbo jumbo. He was saying that salvation comes to you and me when the King of the Kingdom of God comes to live inside us. Robert Boyd Munger wrote a booklet entitled, "My heart, Christ's home." It describes how salvation is you inviting Jesus:

- To come into your life just as if He was coming to live in your home.
- Into every room in your home, even into the hall cupboard where you keep your skeletons!

But once you realise that it is the owner not the guest who cleans the house, you realise that Jesus needs to become the owner of your house. So you willingly transfer the title deed to Him. Jesus is no longer a resident. He becomes the president! That is what it means to surrender to the Lordship of Christ.

Jesus died on the cross so that we can die to ourselves and He can live in us. There is a key verse in Galatians 2 describing all of this. Paul described his life with these words:

"I have been crucified with Christ and I no longer live, but Christ lives in me. The life I live in the body, I live by faith in the Son of God, who loved me and gave himself for me." Galatians 2:20

Paul was stating that the essence of the Christian life is this, "Not I, but Christ living in me." Major Thomas describes the difference between religion and being a Christian. He wrote:

"There are few things quite so boring as being religious, but there is nothing quite so exciting as being a Christian! Most folks have never discovered the difference between the one and the other. There are those who sincerely try to live a life they do not have because they substitute:

- Religion for God
- Christianity for Christ
- Their own noble endeavours for the energy, joy and power of the Holy Spirit. They are like lamps without oil, cars without petrol and pens without ink"

Major Thomas summed up with this comment:

"Many folk are baffled at their own impotence in the absence of all that alone can make man functional; for man was so engineered by God that the presence of the

Creator within the creature is indispensable to His humanity."

The Second Personal Application: Security

When your heart is Christ's home, He does not change addresses!

In the Old Testament God's glory and grace were first displayed in the Tabernacle and later in the two Temples. In those days we could say that God had a Temple for His people. Now God has a people for His Temple. In the words of The Message Bible Translation:

"Did not you realise that your body is a sacred place, the home of the Holy Spirit? The physical part of you is not some piece of property belonging to the spiritual part of you. God owns the whole works. So let people see God in and through your body." 1 Corinthians 6:19

The Temple was a place where God displayed His glory and grace and now, as a Christian, your body is the Temple of the Holy Spirit. Paul writes:

"Christ *in* you the hope of glory." Colossians 1:27

If you believe salvation is Jesus coming to dwell in your life, then the only way you could lose your salvation would be for Jesus to leave you. And He has promised:

"Never will I leave you;
 Never will I forsake you." Hebrews 13:5

David prayed in Psalm 51:

"Do not... take your Holy Spirit from me" Psalm 51:11

In Old Testament times, what David feared was a possibility because the Spirit of God would at times come on and in people and then leave them. We read a clear illustration of this in the story of Samson. Samson's phenomenal strength came from the Spirit of God and not from his long uncut hair. His hair was a symbol of his commitment to God. Judges 14 states:

"the Spirit of the Lord came upon him in power." Judges 14:19

That phrase recurs several times. Only when that happened did he have the strength to fight and defeat the Philistines. After Delilah cut his hair, the Philistines attacked him. Samson jumped up to fight them off as he had always done but we read these sad words:

"But he did not know that the Lord had left him." Judges 16:20

And the Philistines captured him!

In Old Testament times the Spirit of God would come and go but when Jesus talked to His disciples about sending the Holy Spirit to represent Him, He said:

"The Holy Spirit will be with you forever...he lives with you and shall be in you. I will not leave you as orphans; I will come to you." John 14:17-18

As a Christian you are indwelt by the risen Christ. You never need to pray those words of David, "Do not take your Holy Spirit from me." Christ has come to live in your heart and you are His permanent residence!

Christ in you gives you security!

The Third Personal Application: Strength

- Frustration is trying to DO things FOR Jesus.
- Fullness is allowing Jesus to LIVE through you!

Allowing Jesus to live in you does not make you passive. You will find yourself working harder than ever but you will be working in HIS strength and not your own. Notice what Paul wrote about this strength in Colossians 1:

"To this end I labour, struggling with all his energy, which so powerfully works in me." Colossians 1:29

I need to ask you an important question. Which do you think will produce the best result:

- Work done in your energy?
- Work done in His energy?

Paul refers to this secret power again when he wrote:

"It is God who works in you to will and to act according to his good purpose." Philippians 2:13.

A frustrated person is someone who tries to obey God or serve God using their own feeble energy. We all have a tendency to operate in our own strength. Some Christians are continually worn out because they are using up all their energy trying hard to do what can only be done with God's energy. Unfortunately, some are being taught and encouraged to use all their abilities for God and to give Him their very best efforts. This teaching is not new.

One old hymn states:

"Give of your best to the master,
Give of the strength of your youth.
Throw your soul's fresh glowing ardour;
Into the battle for truth.

Jesus has set the example,
Dauntless was he young and brave.
Give him your loyal devotion;
Give him the best that you have."

Now I am sure the writer meant well but the Christian life is not about following the example of Jesus. It is not about giving our best. It is about surrendering our all to Him. My best, even in the strength of my youth, does not measure up to His normal in me!

Major Thomas makes these points in his book The Mystery of Godliness.

Godliness IS NOT:

- Your capacity to imitate God but the consequence of His capacity to reproduce Himself in you.
- Not self-righteousness but Christ righteousness.
- It is not inactivity but Christ-activity.

Godliness IS:

- God in action accomplishing His purpose through human personality—never reducing man to the status of a cabbage but exalting man to the stature of king!

I became a Christian when I was in my teenage years but I did not truly discover the secret to living the Christian life until sometime later. I realised that I could not live the Christian life in my own strength but these seven words changed my life:

CHRIST IN YOU—THE HOPE OF GLORY

Each year it is my privilege to teach at Torchbearer Schools in the UK and mainland Europe, the very schools that Major Thomas founded under God.

Once I began to understand that Jesus lives in me, wants to love people through me, forgive people through me and encourage people through me, it made a huge difference in my life. Instead of trying to imitate the life of Jesus, which I found to be impossible, I started learning to simply abide in Jesus. I am still learning and there are many times when I still try to operate in my own strength. If I have been a blessing to anyone by what I have said, done or written, that was not me. That was Christ in me, the hope of glory.

I heard Stuart Briscoe say that he went through four stages in coming to this same understanding:

- When he first became a Christian he said:

    "This is easy! All I have to do is to repent and ask Jesus to come into my heart—no problem."

- He began to learn what Jesus expected of him and his view of this second stage was:
  "This is difficult!"
  He found it was not as easy as he first thought.
- Stage three was when he admitted:
  "This is impossible!"
  After that confession, he discovered this secret:
  CHRIST IN YOU—THE HOPE OF GLORY
- His comment on stage four was:
  "This is exciting!"

What stage are you in now? Are you looking for something that enables you to rejoice even when you go through the toughest times of life? The answer is found in seven life changing words:

CHRIST IN YOU—THE HOPE OF GLORY

Are you looking for the world's greatest secret, a secret that was hidden for many centuries? The mystery is revealed in seven powerful words:

CHRIST IN YOU—THE HOPE OF GLORY

Do you desire to be complete in every aspect of your personality? Are you tired of trying to live by a "Thou shalts" and "Thou shalt nots" mentality? Here is the secret you need to live by:

CHRIST IN YOU—THE HOPE OF GLORY

So now you know history's greatest mystery.

Chapter 2

How To Catch Sight of God's Will

One of the most popular statements in Christian circles over the past years has been that God loves you and He has a wonderful plan for your life. That is a happy, reassuring thought but a lot of Christians are wondering why God is not telling them what His plan for them is?

You might have followed all the steps that you have been taught as to how to find God's will because you wanted to know:

- Who to marry
- Where to go to college
- Whether to invest in a particular company
- How much to give to the church building fund

Do you lack the certainty that you are making the decisions God wants you to make? Are other Christians claiming that they prayed about this or that and God showed them what to do? You ask me what you are missing. I suspect that you may not be missing anything. You may be suffering from unnecessary frustration and guilt because other Christians are claiming they have something you do not have when the fact is that they do not have it either. They claim they have it because they think that Christians are supposed to have it.

In Acts we read about Paul's decision to visit Jerusalem and there was a disagreement among the believers as to whether he had made the right decision. As you read the verses, look for the different ways in which they try to determine God's Will in the matter.

Paul says:

"And now, compelled by the Spirit, I am going to Jerusalem, not knowing what will happen to me there. I only know that in every city the Holy Spirit warns me that prison and hardships are facing me. However, I consider my life worth nothing to me, if only I may finish the race and complete the task the Lord Jesus has given me — the task of testifying to the gospel of God's grace. Acts 20:22-24

Paul's companion Luke writes:

After we had torn ourselves away from them, we put out to sea and sailed straight to Cos. The next day we went to Rhodes and from there to Patara. We found a ship crossing over to Phoenicia, went on board and set sail. After sighting Cyprus and passing to the south of it, we sailed on to Syria. We landed at Tyre, where our ship was to unload its cargo. Finding the disciples there, we stayed with them seven days. Through the Spirit they urged Paul not to go on to Jerusalem. But when our time was up, we left and continued on our way. All the disciples and their wives and children accompanied us out of the city, and there on the beach we knelt to pray. After saying good-bye to each other, we went aboard the ship, and they returned home. We continued our voyage from Tyre and landed at Ptolemais, where we greeted the brothers and stayed with them for a day. Leaving the next day, we reached Caesarea and stayed at the house of Philip the evangelist, one of the Seven. He had four unmarried daughters who prophesied. After we had been there a number of days, a prophet named Agabus came down from Judea. Coming over to us, he took Paul's belt, tied his own hands and feet with it and said, "The Holy Spirit says, 'In this way the Jews of Jerusalem will bind the owner of this belt and will hand him over to the Gentiles.'" When we heard this, we and the people there pleaded with Paul not to go up to Jerusalem. Then Paul answered, "Why are you weeping and breaking my heart? I am ready not only to be bound, but also to die in Jerusalem for the name of the Lord Jesus." When he would not be dissuaded, we gave up and said,

"The Lord's will be done." Acts 21:1-14

The common thread throughout these verses is the interaction by various groups on Paul's decision:

- Acts 20:22. Paul was determined to go, claiming he was compelled by the Spirit
- Acts 21:4. Fellow believers in Tyre, also speaking by the Spirit, urged Paul not to go.

How can the Holy Spirit tell Paul one thing and at the same time tell other Christians something else? They left Tyre and arrived at Caesarea. Paul stayed with Philip and a prophet named Agabus came from Judea and passed on the Holy Spirit's warning. We read in:

- Acts 21:11 that Agabus used an object lesson to warn Paul what would happen if he visited Jerusalem. Agabus was opposed to Paul's decision.
- Acts 21:12 that Paul's companion, Luke, also begged him not to visit Jerusalem. Luke's use of the word "we" probably includes Philip, his four daughters and the rest of Paul's travelling companions.
- Acts 21:12 also indicates that others, presumably Caesarean Christians, also begged him not to go.

So in these verses we have at least six individuals or groups who are in agreement. Some of them speak by the Holy Spirit. They say to Paul, "Do not go." And what was Paul's response? "I am going."

The key verse is verse 14. Luke writes what they all agreed when Paul could not be dissuaded from going:

"The Lord's will be done." Acts 21:14

We have Paul on one side and a whole group of Christians on the other side. Both sides sincerely desire to know the Will of God on the issue of whether or not Paul should visit Jerusalem. Paul was convinced that he should. They were equally convinced that he should not.

I am not so interested with whether Paul's decision was right or wrong as I am with the way in which his decision was made.

How did Paul decide that it was the Will of God for him to visit Jerusalem and the others decide that it was not? And what did the others mean when they said:

"The Lord's will be done?"

The Will of God

The first thing we need to do is to establish what this phrase means. People can mean at least three distinctly different things when they speak of the Will of God:

- God's Sovereign Will
- God's Moral Will
- God's Individual Will

First: God's Sovereign Will

This is God's undisclosed plan for the universe that determines everything that happens. There are many Scriptures referring to this in both the Old and New Testaments. For instance:

"The lot is cast into the lap, but its EVERY DECISION is from the Lord" Proverbs 16:33

[God] "...works ALL THINGS after the counsel of His will". Ephesians 1:11

The emphasis of these and other verses indicates that God's Sovereign Will includes everything that happens.

Now, I think we can demonstrate biblically that God has a Sovereign Will but we cannot know what it is until it has happened. It is undisclosed except for those prophetic events that God chooses to reveal. So God's Sovereign Will cannot be used by us in making decisions.

There are some Christians who do not believe that God has a Sovereign Will. They believe that God may know in advance what is going to happen but that He does not sovereignly will it to happen. In other words, God has foreknowledge but He does not predetermine what will happen. I think this is largely a matter of playing with words because it is obvious to me that if God foreknows what will happen, it cannot not happen. If it does not happen, then God did not know it!

So I consider that there is no practical difference between foreknowledge and predestination. However, there is a relatively recent view that has become popular in certain evangelical circles known as the Openness of God. This view holds that God does not have complete foreknowledge because He cannot know in advance the decisions of free mortal creatures. I believe this view is wrong. However, even though I affirm my belief in the Sovereign Will of God, I am neither a fatalist nor a determinist. I cannot accept that we are mere puppets on a string.

God's Sovereign Will has two aspects. They are God's:

- Active or Direct Will
- Permissive Will

Some things God actively and directly brings to pass. Other things, like sin for example, God permits to happen. This is a very biblical distinction but either way, God's plan for the universe covers everything and nothing happens that is outside His Sovereign Will.

Second: God's Moral Will

Another aspect of the Will of God is His Moral Will which is His revealed instructions in the Bible as to how people ought to behave. In other words, God's Moral Will equals His desires. God's Sovereign Will includes everything that happens but His Moral Will includes only what He wants to happen. Obviously there is going to be a difference because what God's desires clearly does not always happen. Let me give you an example from First Thessalonians. We are exhorted by Paul to:

"give thanks in all circumstances, for this is God's will for you in Christ Jesus." 1Thessalonians 5:18

It is God's Moral Will or His desire that we should give thanks but it is not His Sovereign Will because sometimes we do not. Then again in First Thessalonians Paul writes:

"It is God's will that you should be sanctified: that you should avoid sexual immorality..." 1Thessalonians 4:3

Once again Paul is writing about God's Moral Will and not His Sovereign Will because regrettably, some Christians do not abstain from sexual sins.

Let us consider a negative example of this. Peter writes:

"He doesn't want anyone to be destroyed. Instead, he wants all people to turn away from their sins." 2Peter 3:9

Universalists believe that everyone will go to heaven. They make the mistake of thinking that Peter was referring to God's Sovereign Will and conclude that no one will perish. But it is clear from the Bible that the unrighteous will perish and that is God's Sovereign Will. God's desire that they repent and not perish is His Moral Will. This is also known God's General or Revealed Will because it has been revealed to everyone. Some of God's Moral Will has been revealed to our consciences. Paul mentions this in Romans:

"...their consciences also bearing witness" Romans 2:15

We can only find all of God's Moral Will in the Bible.

Third: God's Individual Will

There are Christians who speak of yet another, a third Will of God, which they call God's Individual Will. This is the ideal, detailed life plan that God has uniquely designed for every believer and which it is our duty to discern and follow.

They consider that this wonderful plan for our lives impacts upon every decision that we make and it is the basis of God's daily guidance for our lives. It can be referred to as either:

- God's Specific Will
- God's Perfect Will

We can understand the expression God's Specific Will but the expression "God's Perfect Will" is a little confusing because God's Sovereign Will and God's Moral Will are also perfect. What they mean by "perfect" is that this Will of God is "perfect for us" and if we miss it, we have to settle for second best or worse.

The process of finding God's Individual Will might be likened to aiming for the Bull's Eye on a target. If you do not hit it, you have missed God's best for you. But God is gracious and He will not wipe you out just because you missed the Bull's Eye. He will give you some points for getting close but it follows that you will never have a perfect score. For example, if you marry someone other than the partner God chose for you, then your chance of hitting the Bull's Eye is over. If you let Him, God will help you make the best of the bad choice you made. Even His second best is good, though perhaps not great.

Perhaps you have already sensed that I feel there is something wrong with this concept of the Individual Will of God. Before I challenge it, let me tell you about three methods that many have traditionally been taught to discern God's Individual Will for them:

- God's Road Signs.
- The Fleece.
- A direct word from the Lord

Method One: God's Road Signs

Many have been taught that God has provided road signs such as the Scripture, common sense, prayer, circumstances and godly counsel. If and when these signs all line up, then we can be quite sure that we are in the centre of God's Individual Will regarding a particular decision.

If these road signs do not all line up or if we still are not sure, an alternative way of finding God's Individual Will would be for us to "put out a fleece."

Method Two: The Fleece

This idea comes from an Old Testament story that we read about in Judges Chapter 6. Gideon ascertained God's Will in a difficult situation by putting a sheep's fleece out at night and praying that the next morning it would be wet and the ground dry. It was! He did it again and asked for the reverse. The next morning the fleece was dry and the ground was wet.

God used that strange method of speaking to Gideon and many have borrowed it for their own situations. They ask God to speak through a providential sign that they specify beforehand. Unfortunately, it is easy to be "fleeced by a fleece" and I would not recommend this method as a way of determining God's Will. Gideon's requests for confirmation of God's Will and God's responses to him are unique in Scripture but so were the circumstances. Gideon was dealing with his problem from a pagan perspective.

Usually "the fleece method" does not convince us because we do not usually ask for something too spectacular. It is often something like, "Lord, please give me a phone call by 9 o'clock tomorrow morning, then I will know it is Your Will." Why not ask for snow in summer? That would be a bit more conclusive!

Method Three: A direct word from the Lord

There are some people who have an even quicker way of determining God's Individual Will. They get a direct word from the Lord. They are the ones who say words like, "The Lord told me to do such and such," or "The Spirit led me to do this."

Author and Bible Teacher Jon Ortberg recounts the story of how he put a pile of papers, including his schedule, on top of his car and drove off. Later, realising his mistake, he backtracked on his journey but it was hopeless trying to find his papers. Suddenly a lady drove up and said, "Are you looking for these?" and showed him his files. He thanked her and she said, "The Holy Spirit told me they were yours. Do you believe in the Holy Spirit?" He smiled and said, "I certainly do now!"

Of course this kind of thing can and does happen but I believe that such claims are often carelessly made in an effort to clothe human decisions in a spiritual aura. Instead of saying, "I decided to do such and such," we opt to say, "The Lord led me to do such and such," especially if the decision has obvious spiritual implications. Rarely do you hear a pastor say, "I decided to turn down the call to that Church." He will almost always say, "The Lord closed the door to that option." That sounds so much more spiritual!

I need to challenge this concept because I believe that some Christians have misunderstood what the Bible teaches. However before going further I need to make it clear that I do not doubt that God gives direct guidance to some people on some occasions.

The two real issues are these:

- Does God have an Individual Will for each of our lives, a Bull's Eye which we must hit if we do not want to settle for less than His best?
- Do the Scriptures support the concept of God's Individual Will?

Let me make these points clear:

- The biblical passages and examples that are used to support the idea that God has an Individual Will for each of us fall far short of doing so.
- It is certainly correct that some of the prophets and apostles received very specific and direct leading from the Lord.
  - Paul, for example, was at times directed to certain places and forbidden to go to others.
- If you examine the New Testament examples of individual guidance carefully, you will discover that nearly all of them have a direct bearing on the spread of the Gospel.
- One looks in vain for examples of specific guidance from God on the ordinary, yet vitally important, decisions of life that involve:
  - Marriage and family
  - Schools and careers
  - Employment, housing and money.

There are three passages of Scripture which advocates of the "God's Individual Will" concept refer to. Initially, particularly when these passages are read out of context, they do appear to support the concept so let us consider the three passages:

First: Proverbs 3:5-6

"Trust in the LORD with all your heart and lean not on your own understanding; in all your ways acknowledge him, and he will make your paths straight." Proverbs 3:5-6. NIV

Virtually every modern translation of the Bible has correctly translated these verses so that they reflect the original Hebrew. The Authorised or King James Version of the Bible uses the phrase 'direct your paths' but the correct translation is, "make your paths straight." The Hebrew word for "path" describes the general course or fortunes of life. The Hebrew meaning is, "He shall make the course of your life successful."

These two verses do not state, nor even suggest, that God will "make the course of your life successful" by specifically guiding you on an individual path that has been marked out by God for you.

Second: Psalm 32:8

I will instruct you and teach you in the way you should go; I will counsel you and watch over you. Psalms 32:8

It is assumed by some translators and others that it is the Lord who speaks in verse 8. However, this Psalm is a Psalm of David and it is clearly David who writes the first seven verses and verses 10 to the end. We should therefore hesitate before assuming that the Lord speaks the words in verses 8 and 9. But even if it is the Lord who speaks in verse 8, the verse still does not teach the concept of God's Individual Will. The Hebrew translated "counsel" and "the way you should go" refers to God's Moral Will rather than to God's Individual Will. So whether it is the Lord or David speaking, we are simply urged to follow God's Moral Will.

Third: Isaiah 30:20-21

Although the Lord gives you the bread of adversity and the water of affliction, your teachers will be hidden no more; with your own eyes you will see them. Whether you turn to the right or to the left, your ears will hear a voice behind you, saying, "This is the way; walk in it." Isaiah 30:20-21

A few modern translations capitalise the word "teacher" to make it refer to God. For example, The NASU reads: "He, your Teacher will no longer hide Himself." This cannot be correct because in the Hebrew the word "teacher" is plural. The NIV and TNIV correctly translate the word "teachers." These teachers were the prophets. They would come out of hiding where they had been for their own safety.

The 'eyes' and 'ears' are literal because these prophets would then be seen and heard. Furthermore, the reference to "the way" indicates God's Moral Will from which Israel had strayed. The prophets would seek to recall the people whenever they strayed from the straight and narrow way and turned to the right or to the left.

We have considered the three passages of Scripture referred to above to show that they do not teach that God has an Individual Will for our lives. We must next consider experience.

Experience

Does experience support the concept of God's Individual Will? It is my view that it does not. I do not think anyone consistently practices this approach to find God's Will for their lives. All abandon it at some point. Do you seek to find God's Perfect Will for you about the:

- Clothes you buy?
- Food you buy?
- Routes you drive?

Of course not! Neither do I. The point is simply this. The only time we talk about finding God's Perfect Will is in regard to major decisions. For minor decisions you and I are content to use a number of factors such as:

- The Bible
- Our common sense, experience, desires, instinct and the like.
- The advice of others, even strangers.

I have two questions for you:

Question One: Why are the factors that we all use for the minor decisions of life, inadequate to decide the major decisions of life?
My Answer: They are.

Question Two: Is the reason why Christians seek God's Perfect Will in the major decisions of their lives because they do not want to assume personal responsibility for those decisions?
My Answer: To put it bluntly, yes. Many do not want to accept personal blame if the decisions are wrong. So they would like God to make major decisions for them.

God wants to promote maturity in us and He wants us to learn how to make wise decisions. It seems to me that when we are faced with several options that are all within God's Moral Will, we should not worry about missing some imaginary Bull's Eye. Instead we should rejoice and be thankful to God that we have choices.

This story about an unemployed man illustrates my point. He had three job offers. He asked me to pray for him. Because he did not want to miss God's Will, he wanted the Lord to close the doors to the two jobs He did not want him to have. I asked him if any of the jobs was for a crime syndicate or a liquor store. He answered that they were all legitimate jobs that would take care of his family. Why then, I asked him, did he want any of the doors closed?

Do you know why he asked me to pray? He neither wanted to make the decision nor accept responsibility for the consequences if it turned out to be wrong. Do not misunderstand me. My point is not that we should leave God out of our decision making process. Quite the opposite! So what do I consider he should have done when he received three job offers? He should have:

- Thanked God for the options available to him especially as so many were at the time seeking employment.
- Examined the Scriptures for any evidence that God's moral law might be violated by any of his options.
- Prayed that God would help him not to overlook any relevant facts.
- Prayed that God would help him to evaluate his motives.

They would have been wise things to have done. But to pray that God would make the decision for him by sovereignly closing doors was not a legitimate request.

I imagine that you will want to ask me an important question: "Derek, are you saying that God does not choose a spouse for us?" Yes, that is what I am saying.

God expects us to choose a spouse within the limits of His Moral Law. By the time we have considered the limits that God has given us for our good as Christians, there may only be a small number of suitable people. However few or many there are within that number, God gives us the freedom to choose our own spouse. We must use our heads and our hearts as well as the wisdom that God has given us. Then, we must assume full responsibility for our decision.

How to know God's Will

There are three matters that I want to deal with:

- God's Moral Will
- Is there Freedom of Choice?
- What is The Wisest Choice?

God's Moral Will

God's Moral Will, which is revealed in the Bible, has to be considered as foundational and authoritative. If God has left the decision-making process to us, then there is no substitute for knowing the moral boundaries within which our decisions must be made.

I am convinced that if some Christians spent less time trying to discover God's Individual Will for their lives and more time ascertaining God's Moral Will as revealed in the Bible, their lives would be more productive, happy and pleasing to God.

Is there Freedom of Choice?

Within God's Moral Will there is a large freedom area in which we are both free and responsible to make choices. To put it another way, we have:

Total freedom of choice within God's revealed limits.
Any issue not addressed in the Bible either by commandment or by principle is an area of freedom which God is not going to decide for us. Furthermore, any decision within the freedom area is acceptable to God. One option may be wise and another foolish but a foolish option will not be sinful.

What is The Wisest Choice?

The Bible indicates by doctrine and by example that the normal way to make decisions is to use the wisdom God has made available to all of us.

Consider these two passages, both written by Paul:

".... and where there is no law, there is no transgression."
Romans 4:15

"Everything is permissible"—but not everything is beneficial. "Everything is permissible"—but not everything is constructive." 1Corinthians 10:23

Paul is saying that the only way a person can sin against God is to break one of God's Moral Laws or principles, all of which are in the Bible. However, when Paul wrote to the Corinthians, he challenged them to assess the impact that their decisions might have on others. So where God has not laid down restrictions you are free to do what you want but some choices might be better than others and some choices might be unwise and cause problems for yourself and others.

Let me give you two examples of this freedom of choice. There were problems at Rome and Corinth. These problems might be considered by us today to be minor in nature but they needed to be resolved.

The Problem at Rome

In the church in Rome there was obviously some debate about which day was the most appropriate for communal worship. Remember that some of the Roman believers were ex-pagans and not used to Sunday church! Paul writes:

"One man considers one day more sacred than another; another man considers every day alike. Each one should be fully convinced in his own mind." Romans 14:5

Paul writes that each believer should be fully convinced in his own mind. He does not ask them to pray that they will find God's Will in this matter.

The Problem at Corinth

In his second letter to Corinth about stewardship, Paul writes:

"Each man should give what he has decided in his heart to give, not reluctantly or under compulsion, for God loves a cheerful giver." 2Corinthians 9:7

Paul encourages them to think about their contribution and then give what each has decided in his heart to give. The actual amount that should be given was a personal decision, freely made.

In these verses and many like them the issues at hand are the ordinary decisions of life that believers face regularly. There is no requirement or suggestion that we seek God's Perfect Individual Will or even pray about these specific issues. No, the decision is made by us after we have considered all the options and used the wisdom that God has made available to all of us.

Making wise decisions involves:

- Gleaning information from the Scriptures.
- Reason, experience, counsel, circumstances and strong conviction.
- Prayer.

There may be times when the information available to us yields two equal options. In those circumstances I think St. Augustine's advice is appropriate. He said:

"Love God and do what you please."

John MacArthur said the same thing in a slightly different way:

"If you are saved, Spirit filled and sanctified, then do whatever you want to do."
If our lives are right with God, then what God wants will be what we want too.

I want to make it abundantly clear what I am saying. Within the freedom area, our decisions should not be viewed as "God's first choice" or "God's second best" but simply as either wise or unwise.

Let me return to the case of Paul and his decision to go to Jerusalem we were reading about in Acts 21. Did Paul make a wise decision? I am not sure but I think not because reason, counsel, and circumstances were against it. I suspect he made his decision on emotional grounds, based on his intense love for his Jewish countrymen. Luke and the other believers seem to have made their decision on wisdom grounds. Paul felt compelled by the Spirit to go but he might have been wiser to listen to counsel.

But was it sinful for Paul to go on a visit to Jerusalem? No, for his going violated no moral principle of God's revealed Will. That is why they could all say:

"The Lord's will be done." Acts 21:14

And despite all the problems that Paul had to contend with, God graciously used the Jerusalem visit for good. Paul was shipped off to Rome following his arrest to preach the Gospel in the heart of the Roman Empire.

I have a question for you. Luke, referring to Paul, said:
"And since he would not be persuaded, we fell silent, remarking, 'The will of the Lord be done!'" Acts 21:14

Was Luke referring to God's:

- Individual will?
- Moral will?
- Sovereign will?

As mentioned, I do not accept that God has an individualised plan, the Bull's Eye target concept, for each of us and He did not have one for Paul either. So I cannot accept that Luke was referring to God's Individual Will. However, even if there is such a plan, Luke clearly thought Paul's decision was unwise, so he could not have meant God's Individual Will.

God's Moral Will was not an issue as it was not wrong to go or not to go to Jerusalem.

I believe Luke was referring to God's Sovereign Will. Luke was saying to those who were present. "Though we cannot agree on what is a wise decision for Paul and his wish to visit Jerusalem, we have one thing to fall back upon. God has a wise plan for this universe and in that plan He is able to bring good even out of unwise decisions. The will of the Lord be done!"

I want to ensure that none of you reading this chapter misunderstand my teaching. I am not questioning whether God knows in advance all that I will ever do, nor whether He has willed, either directly or permissively, that it be so. I am only questioning whether God has uniquely designed for me an ideal, detailed life plan, which I must discover if I do not want to settle for second best.

I also believe that God can give specific guidance anytime He chooses to and He does that on occasions for some people. But note this carefully. If and when God does give specific guidance, it must be followed. That guidance would be God's Perfect Will and it would be disobedient not to follow it. But I do not think that is God's normal way of dealing with believers, nor do I consider that any believer should feel in any way spiritually inferior if God does not deal that way with them.

Chapter 3

How To Be Valuable Though Ordinary

There is a programme on UK television that I have watched now and again called *"Antiques Roadshow."* In virtually every programme someone discovers that some item, such as a piece of furniture bought for a few pounds, turns out to be worth a whole lot more and sometimes it could have been worth even more if the owner had not painted or polished it! Other antiques are found in cellars and attics many years after being discarded as valueless. It is not that unusual for treasure to be found in strange places, even in clay jars.

In 1947 a Bedouin boy was throwing rocks into a cave near the Dead Sea. He heard the sounds of breaking pottery. That led to the discovery of the Dead Sea Scrolls, the greatest literary treasure ever. The scrolls include copies of every Old Testament book except Esther and they were all from a date more than a thousand years earlier than previously copies.

Paul uses the metaphor of treasure in clay jars when writing to the Corinthian Christians, telling them that they had a treasure but it was in clay jars. What is the treasure and what are the clay jars?

We will find the answers in Second Corinthians 4:

"Therefore, since through God's mercy we have this ministry, we do not lose heart. Rather, we have renounced secret and shameful ways; we do not use deception, nor do we distort the word of God. On the contrary, by setting forth the truth plainly we commend ourselves to every man's conscience in the sight of God. And even if our gospel is veiled, it is veiled to those who are perishing. The god of this age has blinded the minds of unbelievers, so that they cannot see the light of the gospel of the glory of Christ, who is the image of God. For we do not preach ourselves, but Jesus Christ as Lord, and ourselves as your servants for Jesus' sake. For God, who said, "Let light shine out of darkness," made his light shine in our hearts to give us the light of the knowledge of the glory of God in the face of Christ. But we have this treasure in jars of clay to show that this all-surpassing power is from God and not from us. We are hard pressed on every side, but not crushed; perplexed, but not in despair; persecuted, but not abandoned; struck down, but not destroyed. We always carry around in our body the death of Jesus, so that the life of Jesus may also be revealed in our body. For we who are alive are always being given over to death for Jesus' sake, so that his life may be revealed in our mortal body. So then, death is at work in us, but life is at work in you." 2Corinthians 4:1-12

The overall theme of the passage is the lifestyle of servant leaders. Regrettably, servant leaders seem to be rapidly vanishing today. Churches now seek world-class communicators and dynamic visionaries with chief executive officer capabilities as their leaders, rather than shepherds or servants. You would be surprised at how the "Positions Available" descriptions in advertisements seeking Senior Pastors have changed over the years.

Thirty years ago churches sought a man of integrity and prayer, one who would study the Scriptures, teach well and love people. Today the focus is on leadership issues, coaching, mentoring, teamwork, motivational skills, articulation of vision and of course, management ability.

The time that a pastor spends on administration and management cannot also be spent studying God's Word and looking after the spiritual needs of those who God has placed in his care. In the process of this change something has been lost when it comes to biblical literacy and holy living.

In consequence, sadly the respect that you would have expected there to be for servant leaders has also generally and substantially diminished in the church at the present time. Some are surprised to learn that not all the servant leaders in the early church were respected either. The church at Corinth is a case in point. It appears that some members of the church felt that Paul was not very impressive for someone who claimed to be an Apostle.

Paul had founded the church at Corinth and personally led many of them to Christ but now that he had been gone for a while and they had become accustomed to a new style of leadership, they became quite critical of Paul. Their criticisms, if not so offensive, might have made us smile!

What were they? They complained that Paul:

- Was not very good looking.
- Was not eloquent.
- Did not have the credentials they now required.
- Did not charge for his services which indicated that they were not worth much.
- Was constantly facing persecution and suffering and that sort of thing did not fit with their misguided health-wealth theology.

As we read in the verses, Paul defends himself and his ministry. Note that he writes the first person plural pronoun. He uses the word "we" rather than "I." I think that he wanted to encourage all of us to have the same spiritual characteristics that are required of a servant leader. As we read Chapter 4 let us consider the:

- Character of the Servant Leader.
- Responsibilities of the Servant Leader.
- Ultimate impact of the Faithful Servant Leader.

The Character of The Servant Leader

There are five characteristics of The Servant Leader that I want to consider. The Servant Leader is:

- Spiritually courageous.
- Morally sound.
- Intellectually honest.
- Aware of Satan.
- Faithful in the Gospel.

One: The Servant Leader is Spiritually Courageous

Paul writes in verse 1 that "We do not lose heart." Ministry is tough and it is so easy to give it up. I suppose everyone has at some point been tempted to throw in the towel. Perhaps we have said, "Who needs this? I am only a volunteer and no one seems to appreciate my efforts. I am out of here!" But Paul refers to something that should stop us in our tracks. He writes:

"...since through God's mercy we have this ministry, we do not lose heart." 2Corinthians 4:1

Paul is writing about the ministry of the New Covenant. Maybe if we were under the performance standards of the Old Covenant that I have written about in Chapter 1, Paul could understand us giving up because failure was so common and the results so discouraging. But the New Covenant offers us so much more:

- Hope.
- Forgiveness.
- Power.
- Victory.

- It results in transformed lives!

Therefore, Paul states:

"...we do not lose heart." 2Corinthians 4:1

We remain faithful. Paul did not take any credit for the ministry he had. It was not his idea and he did not earn the right to it through his hard work or exceptional brilliance. Rather it was his through God's mercy. The fact that any of us are able to serve God is a privilege beyond description.

Two: The Servant Leader is Morally Sound

Paul writes in verse 2:

"We have renounced secret and shameful ways."

Sadly, some people use religion for shameful purposes. We have been inundated with reports of priests who have used their positions to prey on children and we are all aware of TV preachers who have become very wealthy through self-promotion. They almost always hide their financial dealings because they do not want to be accountable.

But it is not just the full time professionals who are guilty of secret and shameful behaviour. What about the youth leader who feeds on internet pornography in the privacy of his home or the Sunday School teacher who spends hours reading romance novels or watching trashy soap operas? The servant leader must always be:

- A person of integrity
- Open and transparent
- The same in public as in private.

Three: The Servant Leader is Intellectually Honest

Paul writes in verse 2:

"We do not use deception, nor do we distort the word of God."

Public relations experts, known as spin doctors, have sprung up in recent years. It is their job to highlight the positive aspects and play down the negative aspects of whatever a politician or political party says or does. Hence, we rarely hear politicians say "sorry." Instead, the spin doctors perform their surgery on the truth and then present immoral or dishonest activities to us in the most favourable light.

Sadly, spin doctors have also entered the ministry. They are able to spin anything to make it sound spiritual, even if it is directly opposed to what the Bible teaches. That is why, for example, we have openly sinful ministers claiming that the Bible supports their immoral behaviour and lifestyle.

The Bible can be distorted in less drastic ways too. I find some evangelical Christians manipulating it to protect their favourite doctrines. Paul would not do that.

Paul continues in verse 2:

"On the contrary, by setting forth the truth plainly we commend ourselves to every man's conscience in the sight of God."

This is the opposite of spinning the truth. The church should be a no-spin zone. We should never be guilty of embellishing the truth or dressing it up in language that make us look scholarly.

Truth is not always easy to grasp but our goal must always be to make it as plain as we possibly can. Let me ask you two questions about this. How else:

- Are people's consciences going to be challenged?
- Is the truth going to penetrate their hearts?

Four: The Servant Leader is Aware of Satan

In verses 3-4 Paul writes:

"And even if our gospel is veiled, it is veiled to those who are perishing. The god of this age has blinded the minds of unbelievers, so that they cannot see the light of the Gospel of the glory of Christ, who is the image of God."

A servant leader must be:

- Spiritually courageous.
- Morally sound.
- Intellectually honest.

Let me make this clear. Even if the servant leader has these vital qualities, there is no guarantee that his message will be well received. Paul recognised there is a satanic blindness that prevents some people from seeing the truth of the Gospel. Have you ever wondered why some people refuse to believe the Gospel despite having heard it repeatedly? They live seemingly oblivious to the fact that judgment is coming for everyone who has not accepted the Gospel. Paul attributes this state of affairs to spiritual blindness.

In Chapter 3 Paul mentioned the veil that covered the hearts of the people who followed the Old Covenant. Now he states that unbelievers in general suffer from a spiritual blindness that has satanic origins. "The god of this world" is clearly a reference to Satan. He is treated as a god by his own minions. Because Jesus died on the cross, Satan is a defeated enemy but he is still actively opposed to God and His people and we have to be aware of his deceitful and cunning strategies.

We know that Satan works in a variety of ways on the minds and hearts of unbelievers to the extent that, in the words of verse 4:

"...they cannot see the light of the gospel of the glory of Christ, who is the image of God."

Satan hides from unbelievers the truth of who Jesus is. Satan's fine with unbelievers paying lip service to Jesus as a great teacher, a lover of the poor, even a martyr. But Satan does not want unbelievers to see the beauty of Jesus, His grace, His mercy, His love and especially His forgiveness. This is essentially the same truth that Paul refers to in First Corinthians:

"The man without the Spirit does not accept the things that come from the Spirit of God, for they are foolishness to him, and he cannot understand them, because they are spiritually discerned." 1Corinthians 2:14-15

I have known individuals sit for decades under the teaching of God's Word but they never gave any evidence of responding to it. You perhaps have had the experience of sharing your faith with a family member for many years and yet nothing ever seems to get through to them. I know of many believers who share your frustration, your personal sorrow and prayers.

Let us consider three important questions that Christians ask about this matter.

Question One: Does satanic blindness mean that unbelievers cannot understand the words we use?
Answer: No.

Question Two: Does satanic blindness mean that unbelievers cannot learn spiritual truths?

Answer: No. There are unbelievers who have a wonderful intellectual capacity for biblical studies.

Question 3: If unbelievers cannot see the light of the Gospel because of satanic blindness, does it mean that they are not responsible for their actions?

Answer: No. They are "without excuse" writes Paul in Romans 1:20 because they see enough and know enough to make them responsible. Paul then states:

"Since the creation of the world God's invisible qualities–his eternal power and divine nature–have been clearly seen, being understood from what has been made." Romans 1:20

Paul adds these sad words in the next verse:

"Although they knew God, they neither glorified him as God nor gave thanks to him, but their thinking became futile and their foolish hearts were darkened." Romans 1:21

Unbelievers will be held accountable because:

- They co-operate with Satan in their own spiritual blindness:
  - By exchanging the Glory of God for idols
  - By exchanging the Truth of God for a lie.
- They made decisions along the way that gave Satan a foothold.

- They willingly allowed Satan to tamper with their minds.

The wise Servant Leader will recognise and accept that:

- Satanic blindness will limit the success of his ministry because:
  - He is not competing in the marketplace of human ideas.
  - He is in a spiritual battle that involves supernatural forces.
- His ultimate responsibility is to be faithful.

Five: The Servant Leader is Faithful in The Gospel

Paul wrote in verse 5:

"... we... preach... Jesus Christ as Lord."

Because we recognise the power of Satan, it would be easy to say, "If unbelievers suffer from supernatural blindness, what is the point in witnessing to them?" Such an attitude ignores other factors that might contribute to an unbeliever's spiritual condition. For example, the fact that:

- No one has explained the Gospel to them.
- The Gospel has been explained but not lived out.

I am sure that we can attribute the fact that our neighbours are unchurched to satanic blindness. But if we do not invite unbelievers to outreach events, how can we only blame Satan for their lost condition? In revealing His Will to Ezekiel the Lord said:

"Son of man, I have made you a watchman for the house of Israel; so hear the word I speak and give them warning from me. When I say to a wicked man, 'You will surely die,' and you do not warn him or speak out to dissuade him from his evil ways in order to save his life, that wicked man will die for his sin, and I will hold you accountable for his blood. But if you do warn the wicked man and he does not turn from his wickedness or from his evil ways, he will die for his sin; but you will have saved yourself. Ezekiel 3:17-19

The solemn message is that God does not hold Satan solely accountable for the lost condition of unbelievers. He holds us accountable too. The wise servant leader will recognise the limitations that satanic blindness puts on his ministry but he will not use that as an excuse for failing to share the Gospel. Hence Paul states that our responsibility is to share the Gospel with unbelievers. Why? Because the Gospel is the principal antidote that God has established to deal with satanic blindness.

We have considered five characteristics of the Servant Leader. He is:

- Spiritually courageous.
- Morally sound.
- Intellectually honest.

- Aware of Satan.
- Faithful in The Gospel.

Now let us look at how his character has a vital impact on his responsibilities.

The Responsibilities of the Servant Leader

There are three responsibilities of the Servant Leader that I want to consider. The Servant Leader:

- Puts Christ first.
- Trusts God to shine light into the darkness of sin.
- Remains just a clay jar to ensure that God gets all the credit.

The Servant Leader puts Christ first

Paul writes in verse 5:

"For we do not preach ourselves, but Jesus Christ as Lord, and ourselves as your servants for Jesus' sake."

The response of some leaders to the problem of satanic blindness is to try new techniques and methodologies. They consider better advertising, new ways of worship or a new cultural approach. These initiatives may increase the audience but since satanic blindness is supernatural, only a supernatural power can remove it.

That power is found only in Jesus Christ. That is why Paul says we must preach Christ, not ourselves.

There are preachers who constantly tell stories about themselves and their families. Their children say the cutest things. They have the perfect marriage that seems to be the perfect illustration of almost any spiritual truth. There are also people who are so full of themselves that they only talk about themselves. They leave no room for Jesus.

In First Corinthians Paul wrote:

"For I resolved to know nothing while I was with you except Jesus Christ and him crucified." 1Corinthians 2:2

For Paul, the subject of Jesus and the cross was so central to his teaching that every other subject he taught the Corinthians led back to it. The words most on Paul's lips were, "Jesus is Lord." And if Jesus is Lord, then Paul is His servant. Paul is not into impressing others but rather serving them.

The Servant Leader trusts God to shine light into the darkness of sin

In verse 6 Paul writes:

"For God, who said, "Let light shine out of darkness," made his light shine in our hearts to give us the light of the knowledge of the glory of God in the face of Christ."

Paul goes back to Genesis 1. He states that the God who at the dawn of creation dispelled the darkness, is the same God who causes spiritual light to drive out the darkness of sin and unbelief from the hearts of men. It took the miracle of creation to separate light from darkness and it takes the miracle of a new creation to bring an individual out of spiritual darkness into the light. There are three forces at work when someone comes to faith in Christ. They are not equal forces by any means but they are all active:

Force One: Satan blinds.
Force Two: We proclaim.
Force Three: God turns on the light.
We must both realise and accept what we can and cannot do to bring an unbeliever to faith in Christ:

- We cannot deactivate Force One because it is Satan personally who has blinded unbelievers.
- We cannot activate Force Three because only God personally can turn on the light.
- But we are Force Two and we can and are responsible for proclaiming the truth.

The Servant Leader remains just a clay jar to ensure that God gets all the credit.

Paul writes in verse 7:

"But we have this treasure in jars of clay."

So far we are happy to agree with Paul. We like his selfless attitude and agree with his philosophy of ministry. But he comes to a topic that we do not relate to nearly as well. It is humility. Paul stresses the humble position of the true Servant Leader as opposed to the strong, dynamic, chief executive officer model of leadership the Corinthians wanted.

Verse 7 refers to the contrast of treasure and clay jars but what is the treasure? I think verse 6 contains the nearest that we can get to it. Paul writes:

"...the light of the knowledge of the glory of God in the face of Christ."

That is the treasure! And God has chosen not to deposit that knowledge in the brilliant or the noble and powerful minds of our culture. Instead, He has placed it in clay jars that represent those ordinary earthen vessels that are so symbolic of weak, inadequate and sometimes foolish human beings.

Why has God put something that is so valuable, and of vital importance to Him, into easily broken vessels? Paul tells us why in verse 7:

"to show that this all-surpassing power is from God and not from us."

We use power to:

- Destroy.
- Tear things apart.
- Blast, explode and crush.

But this all-surpassing power from God, in total contrast to man's power:

- Unites and gathers.
- Harmonises.
- Removes divisions and barriers that have caused separation.

This all-surpassing power from God:

- Does not make superficial, external adjustments.
- Works from within.
- Produces permanent transformations and eternal results.

Because I want to emphasise how humble the truth that we are considering in verse 7 should make us, I want you to answer this question before reading on. Do you know any other power like this all-surpassing power from God? It is absolutely unrivalled and yet, amazingly, it is placed into the hands of ordinary fragile clay jars like you and me. This is the same point that Paul makes in First Corinthians:

"God chose the foolish things of the world to shame the wise; God chose the weak things of the world to shame the strong. He chose the lowly things of this world and the despised things-and the things that are not–to nullify the things that are, so that no one may boast before him."1Corinthians 1:27-29

Paul's detractors at Corinth thought, "How can you hope to make an impression with the Gospel unless the spokesman himself is impressive?" But Paul realised that God's clay jar plan was far superior. Why? Because it would guard against the danger that the credit that is due to God would go to one of His human instruments instead. Whenever we start thinking that we are pretty important, particularly gifted and eminently successful, it would be wise to come back to this verse. We are just clay jars. Paul is here concerned to show how the grace of God is magnified when His human instruments are at their weakest.

Maybe you are familiar with the words of Paul that we read in verses 8 and 9:

"We are hard pressed on every side, but not crushed; perplexed, but not in despair; persecuted, but not abandoned; struck down, but not destroyed."

I want you to understand what Paul is telling us in these verses. Paul did not write them to display his own perseverance and courage. He wrote them to display

God's power and providence. God did not stop the trials and the persecution that Paul experiences during his life of faithful service but God put limits on those ordeals.

Remember Job? He endured the attempts of his so-called friends to explain his suffering. He engaged in some personal justification. God challenged him regarding his attitude. We read in Job:

"Then the LORD answered Job out of the storm. He said:"Who is this that darkens my counsel with words without knowledge? Brace yourself like a man; I will question you, and you shall answer me. "Where were you when I laid the earth's foundation? Tell me, if you understand. Who marked off its dimensions? Surely you know! Who stretched a measuring line across it? On what were its footings set, or who laid its cornerstone-while the morning stars sang together and all the angels shouted for joy? "Who shut up the sea behind doors when it burst forth from the womb, when I made the clouds its garment and wrapped it in thick darkness, when I fixed limits for it and set its doors and bars in place, when I said, 'This far you may come and no farther; here is where your proud waves halt'?" Job 38:1-11

Read again the last sentence. We know of the enormous power of cyclones and the floods that they cause. Waves seem out of control but they are not. God has fixed limits for the waves of the sea and He says to any trial that His children face, "This far you may come and no farther." No trials can touch us that have not passed through the hands of our Heavenly Father.

Let us go back to the words of Paul in verses 8 and 9. He notes that experiences have effects on us and accepts that there are some experiences that could have serious consequences for us. So Paul asks searching questions about the various experiences that God allows us to go through and states their effects on us.

Paul's words tell us that he was a hard-headed realist with no romantic illusions about his service for God. Far from depicting himself as a spiritual superhero blazing a trail of success like a comet across the first-century sky, Paul portrayed himself as a groggy fighter. He staggers from a succession of near-lethal blows and is surprised to find that he is still on his feet. But Paul knows that it is only by the grace of God that he is standing.

The Impact of The Faithful Servant Leader

His impact is best expressed this way: As the faithful Servant Leader experiences the death or suffering of Jesus, he reveals the life of Jesus to unbelievers.

Paul expresses this truth in three consecutive statements that are found in verses 10 to 12. Each statement begins with death and end with life:

Verse 10: We always carry around in our body the death of Jesus, so that the life of Jesus may also be revealed in our body.

Verse 11: For we who are alive are always being given over to death for Jesus' sake, so that his life may be revealed in our mortal body.

Verse 12: So then, death is at work in us, but life is at work in you.

The essential point Paul is making in each of these statements is that the Servant Leader will one day undergo decay and death. Not only will we suffer the normal effects of the ageing process, we can additionally expect suffering, persecution and even death for the sake of the Gospel. These trials, however, can be spiritually productive in the lives of others. As we accept suffering and respond to it in godly ways, those around us see Jesus and are drawn to Him. That makes the hard times worthwhile.

As you spend time thinking these verses through and I conclude the chapter, may I ask you two further questions to challenge you in your service for God?

- Question One: Do you ever complain to God that He has not given you a better clay jar?
- Question Two: Are you ever jealous of the style, colour or shape of other clay jars that you meet?

God wants to get our eyes off the clay jars so that we can appreciate the treasure they contain.

God has given us the light of the knowledge of the glory of God in the face of Christ and He wants us to share that knowledge with others. Did you know that Christ wants to get out of your life? Why? Because He wants His presence shining out through your life.

Chapter 4

How To React To Suffering

Elie Wiesel was a survivor of a concentration camp as a child and in later life become a Nobel Laureate. His eyes, deep set and haunting, were enough to tell you he had seen horrors and experienced trauma that defied human articulation. They could only be known by being felt and you felt them by looking in his eyes. He asked a student during an individual meeting with him:

- How do you cope with God?
- Why life?
- Why death?
- Why suffering?

For Wiesel, it was not a question of whether God existed or not. It was the fact that God did exist and had allowed atrocities to occur that caused him anguish.

The student did not know what to say. Every word he thought of sounded trite and flimsy because he knew he did not have Wiesel's look in his own eyes. This experience began to push him to the brink of his own understanding of pain and to realise that human suffering is extreme, not just because we suffer, but because, unlike animals, we look for meaning in our suffering. It is that longing for meaning in the midst of incomprehensible, senseless pain that makes us ask:

- Why?
- What is the purpose?
- Why does God allow it?

And those in some ways unanswerable questions increase the suffering we experience.

Many Christians think the two words, "Christian" and "suffering" should not be joined. For many, the label "Christian suffering" sounds out-of-place. They insist a Christian should never have to endure pain and suffering. But the Bible speaks plainly about the reality of suffering in the lives of Christians.

Peter wrote to Christians who were suffering terrible persecution. A fire destroyed two-thirds of Rome. Nero blamed the Christians for the fire and as a result, they were dreadfully persecuted. Peter wrote a letter to encourage them and he addressed the subject of suffering fifteen times in five chapters. We are going to consider First Peter 1:

"In this you greatly rejoice, though now for a little while you may have had to suffer grief in all kinds of trials. These have come so that your faith — of greater worth than gold, which perishes even though refined by fire — may be proved genuine and may result in praise, glory and honour when Jesus Christ is revealed. Though you have not seen him, you love him; and even though you do not see him now, you believe in him and are filled with an inexpressible and glorious joy, for you are receiving the goal of your faith, the salvation of your souls." 1Peter 1:6-9

Peter warns us that even though we are followers of Jesus, we will experience trials. The word "trial" is another word for "trouble" or "tribulation." A trial is a painful experience that, given the choice, we would avoid. But since we are going to face trials, we should learn about what they are and how we should react to suffering. So let us examine four important principles about trials and tribulations:

First Principle: Trials come in a variety of forms.
Second Principle: Trials reveal the purity of our faith.
Third Principle: Trials force us to focus on Jesus.
Fourth Principle: Trials can produce glorious joy.

First Principle: Trials come in a variety of forms

Peter writes in verse 6:

"For a little while you may have had to suffer grief in all kinds of trials."

73

It is important to understand that a trial is not a temptation. James writes about both trials and temptations and he makes a distinction between them.

These are the five differences:

- A temptation is devised by Satan to make us sin.
  A trial is allowed by God to let us shine.
- A temptation is designed to drive us away from God
  A trial is designed to draw us closer to God
- A temptation will weaken us.
  A trial will strengthen us.
- A temptation is never unbearable. The Bible says we will never be tempted beyond what we can bear.
  A trial is often beyond our own ability to endure.
- A temptation must be resisted.
  A trial should be embraced.

Sadly we often resist God's trials and embrace Satan's temptations!

Peter writes that we will suffer "all kinds of trials." That is a phrase that means "variegated colours." It is like a stained glass window comprised of hundreds of different coloured pieces of glass. An isolated trial is like one small piece from that window that may not impress us. When we consider all the trials that we will experience, we will realise that God is making our lives into something that is both beautiful and valuable.

You may face a financial trial when money problems arise or a physical trial when a doctor confirms an illness and your life is immediately changed. Some have matrimonial trials or trials at work. There are many colour variations in the universe and you may expect that kind of variety in trials and tribulations.

Job was a God-fearing man who lived in Old Testament days. He had many blessings. Satan told God that if Job lost his blessings, he would also lose his faith. God allowed Satan to test Job but God set a limit as to what Satan could do. Trials and tribulations came into Job's life and he lost his wealth, family and health. Job made this observation that you can read in Job 5:7

"Man is born to trouble as surely as sparks fly upward."

It is the nature of fire to throw sparks upward and it is part of our nature to experience pain and suffering. When Job's troubles started his wife and friends told him to:

"...curse God and die." Job 2:9.

But, ignoring that foolish advice, Job came to a point where he could boldly say:

"I know that my redeemer lives! And I shall see Him someday!" Job 19:25

Satan was proved wrong. Job passed the test.

When you are being tested, it is important to remember that God set a limit as to what Satan could do to Job. In the same way, our trials may come from Satan but they are filtered by God. When you make filtered coffee you put a filter in the coffee maker to avoid coffee grounds in your cup. It is good to know that all your trials have to pass through the filter of God's grace and mercy and the filter of His omnipotence. What painful experience are you facing right now? Would it make a difference if you knew it was a test? How would you respond if you were going through the same test Job faced?

Suffering for a Christian is like that Emergency Broadcasting System Announcement you hear on the TV and radio when you are in America. They break into the program and you hear the words, "This is a test. This is only a test." When you face trials and tribulations, remember those words and say to yourself:

This is a test. This is only a test!

Second Principle: Trials reveal the purity of our faith

Peter writes in verse 7:

"These have come so that your faith–of greater worth than gold, which perishes even though refined by fire–may be proved genuine."

Gold is a fascinating commodity. It is valuable on earth because it is rare but John writes that in heaven, the street is made of gold! Peter writes that there is something we possess that is of greater value than gold. It is our faith. Like gold, our faith is refined by fire but for us, it is the fire of suffering.

Gold is found embedded in rock so it must first be extracted and then refined. Crushed rock is placed in a crucible and heated. As the gold melts, it is removed. Gold can be combined with other metals. 18 carat gold contains 75% gold compared to pure gold which is 24 carat. Costume jewellery looks great but it is only painted with gold. Over the years the gold paint wears off and the base metal is revealed.

God refines our faith to prove our faith is genuine and to purify it. It is only in the fire of suffering that you discover whether your faith is genuine or a cheap imitation. When, to quote from Porgy and Bess, it is 'summertime and the living is easy," it is also easy to say that you have faith. It really is during the tough times that your faith is proved.

The Bible not only compares our faith to gold. It also mentions silver. God is the refiner and He sometimes turns up the heat so that our faith can be purified. Like both gold and silver, our faith contains impurities and it is through the fire of suffering that our faith is purified. In Isaiah 48 God says:

"See I have refined you, though not as silver; I have tested you in the furnace of affliction." Isaiah 48:10

Is your faith the real thing? Nobody likes to go through "the furnace of affliction" but if your faith is real, this process will make it more valuable.

Recently I read about the experience of a Christian who became ill. Tests revealed he had cancer in his throat, a scary diagnosis for anyone. After surgery he had forty-two painful radiation treatments. He was strapped down to a metal table for thirty minutes while the radiation was directed to different parts of his throat. He was literally going through the fire because the radiation was burning away the affected tissue.

He lost forty pounds and his hair came out in clumps. His throat hurt so badly he could not swallow water without pain medication. He asked himself and had to face these searching questions about his belief in God:

- Was what he had said about his belief in God real?
- Was this belief something he only mentioned when everything was going well?

He discovered at his lowest point that he was not afraid to die. The song that meant so much to him was "I Can Only Imagine" by Mercy Me and it was played during his treatments. He came to understand and appreciate that his worst case scenario was meeting Jesus face to face and that was not scary at all.

His last two checkups have revealed no re-occurrence of the cancer. He wrote that as he looked back on that experience, he had made a valuable discovery. His faith was real, like pure gold. It had been purified. It had become stronger.

Are you facing a furnace of affliction right now? God is not the author of suffering but He can use it. Sickness and disease are the consequences of living in a fallen, sinful world. But when you find yourself in the fire of affliction, remember that God is testing you. Your faith may have impurities in it so God may turn up the heat to get rid of them.

Remember that although the fire is not pleasant, it is proving and purifying your faith. Do not fear that you will be consumed by the fire. God loves you and He is in control. Remember that God may not ignite the fire of affliction but He controls the thermostat! When will God turn down the heat? Only when His refining process is finished.

A silversmith looks into the crucible and watches as the molten silver floats to the top. He knows the silver is pure when he can see a perfect reflection of his face in it. As the refiner, God is looking at you and when He sees the reflection of the character of Jesus in your life, that episode of refining is usually complete.

Third Principle: Trials force us to focus on Jesus

Trials are difficult and the best way to endure them is to look to Jesus who is "the author and perfecter of our faith." Peter makes it clear that although we cannot see Jesus with our human eyes, we can still believe in Him. Peter wrote in verses 7 and 8:

Trials "...have come so that your faith — of greater worth than gold, which perishes even though refined by fire — may be proved genuine and may result in praise, glory and honour when Jesus Christ is revealed. Though you have not seen him, you love him; and even though you do not see him now, you believe in him and are filled with an inexpressible and glorious joy."

If we could see Jesus standing in front of us when we were suffering, it would be easy to believe. But Peter is telling us that we must develop eyes of faith. God has a way of getting our attention when we are suffering as C.S. Lewis discovered after he came through a time of caring for his wife as she was dying of cancer. He wrote:

"God whispers to us in our pleasures but He shouts to us in our pain. Suffering is God's megaphone to awake a sleeping world."

That is why we need to embrace our trials rather than running from them.

We know from John 20 that on the first Easter Sunday evening, Jesus appeared to His disciples in the upper room but Thomas was not there. Later, the disciples told him that Jesus was alive but he did not believe them. Thomas said:

"Unless I can see Him with my eyes and put my fingers in the nail prints and wound in His side I will not believe!" John 20:25

That is why today many refer to him as "Doubting Thomas." A week later Jesus returned and Thomas was present. Jesus approached him and said:

"...Put your finger here; see my hands. Reach out your hand and put it into my side. Stop doubting and believe."
John 20:27

Thomas simply said, "My Lord and my God!" Then Jesus made this profound statement about Thomas and about us. Jesus said to Thomas:

"...Because you have seen me, you have believed; blessed are those who have not seen me and yet have believed!"
John 20:29

That is what Peter is repeating in verse 8. We have not seen Jesus with our human eyes, so we look at Him with eyes of faith.

There is a great story that you can read in Second Chronicles 20 about keeping your eyes on God even though you cannot see Him. Jehoshaphat was King of Judah. He and his small army were surrounded by their enemies. Although the King was scared, he prayed this powerful prayer of faith:

"O our God...we have no power to face this vast army that is attacking us. We do not know what to do, but our eyes are upon you." 2Chronicles 20:12

Then the King devised an unusual battle plan. He put men on the front line to sing to the Lord and praise Him. As they led that small army into battle they said:

"Give thanks to the LORD, for his love endures forever." 2Chronicles 20:21

Then they sang songs of praise to God. The Bible says the LORD set ambushes against the enemy and they started to fight each other until they killed each other. What a powerful lesson for us today! When we face our enemies and difficult situations:

- We must not focus our eyes on the problems.
- We must focus our eyes on God.
- We must deal with our problems with thanks and praise on our lips.

Are you suffering at this moment?

- You must not focus on your problems or pains.
- You must focus your eyes on God.

When you focus on Him, you will want to praise Him. If you do, you will experience God's blessing.

Years ago there was a popular praise song which goes as

follows:

"It's amazing what praising will do.
Hallelujah. Hallelujah!
It's amazing what praising will do!
Hallelujah!
I don't worry when things go wrong.
Jesus fills my heart with a song.
It's amazing what praising will do.
Hallelujah!"

Remember, it is Peter, the big fisherman who wrote these verses. He knew what happened when you took your eyes off Jesus. One night Jesus came walking on the Sea of Galilee to join the disciples who were in a boat. Peter asked Jesus if he could leave the boat and walk to Him on the water. Jesus said, "Come on!" Peter stepped out in faith and started walking on the water. But the Bible says that Peter started to feel the strong wind, became frightened and began to sink. When you take your eyes off Jesus and only look at your difficulties, you are in trouble. If you focus on Jesus, you can walk to victory!

Fourth Principle: Trials can produce glorious joy

In verse 6 Peter writes:

"In this you greatly rejoice."

In verses 8 and 9 Peter writes:

"...You are filled with an inexpressible and glorious joy, for you are receiving the goal of your faith, the salvation of your souls."

Peter repeats that we should rejoice when we face trials and suffering. Rejoicing is not a feeling. It is something that we choose to do or not to do! Rejoicing differentiates us from those who do not know Jesus. We should express joy, even when we are suffering. When you are going through the furnace of affliction, you are forced to depend on God. One reason God allows you to suffer is so you will grasp hold of His power with both hands. It may be that you are suffering because God is trying to teach you that He is all you need.

The promise of God is that we will only suffer for a little while. Even if we suffer for eighty years, that is just a blip on the timeline of eternity. There are plenty of experiences that cause us pain and our eyes often fill up with tears but God promises in eternity that He will wipe all the tears from our eyes. God gives us a great promise in Psalm 30:

"Weeping may remain for a night, but rejoicing comes in the morning." Psalm 30:5

Are you suffering in the dark night of depression and discouragement? You know that the morning is coming but I want you to know that you do not have to wait until it arrives to rejoice. This is so very important. You can rejoice now. Let this acrostic for SUFFER help you:

Step Up For Faith's Eternal Reward

When you suffer, realise that it is a test. Understand that your faith is more valuable than gold and that you are going through a refining process. Focus your eyes on Jesus and even though you do not see Him, trust Him. Then you will be able to rejoice.

Once, when Martin Luther was depressed, his wife entered his study wearing all black. Even her face was covered with a black veil. Naturally Luther asked who had died. She said, "God." Martin Luther responded, "God has not died." She said, "Oh, I thought by the way you were acting that God had died." She wanted to remind him that Jesus is alive and God is in control. It worked. Martin Luther left his bad mood and began to rejoice again.

Those who visit concentration camps see the despair in the eyes of the prisoners as they stare out from the many photographs displayed. In the menaces of such places, as well as in the depths of mental turmoil and the throes of serious illness, people have found Jesus. God's presence is alive even in the darkest pit. I came across a prayer found written on wrapping paper by Allied troops who were liberating prisoners held in a camp. It had been composed by a prisoner who had died before rescue came. It read:

"O Lord, Jesus,
Remember not only the men and women of goodwill,
But also those of ill will.
But do not only remember the suffering they have inflicted on us,
Remember the fruits we bore thanks to this suffering,
Our comradeship, our loyalty, our humility,
The courage, the generosity,
The greatness of heart which has grown out of all this.
And when they come to judgment,
Let all the fruits that we have borne
Be their forgiveness.
Amen, Amen, Amen."

That is such unanswerable proof that there is no depth of pain to which we can go where God's love is not deeper still. You do not have to let suffering and evil have the last word in your life. You can, by the grace of Jesus Christ and the power of the Holy Spirit, choose to love and rejoice.

Chapter 5

How To Smell Right

Anxious because she was to meet her boyfriend's parents for the first time, a young lady took one last look in the mirror. Thinking that her shoes could do with a shine but with little time, she picked up a paper tissue used for the breakfast bacon and wiped her shoes. His parents were very impressed with her. His mother said, "You know, our wonderful little dog is a good judge of character and I can see from the way she is sniffing around your shoes that she really likes you."

The Scriptures do not often ask us to think about our aroma but Paul does just that. He challenges us with what I like to call "the doctrine of smell." It has nothing to do with bacon or how our sinuses are working. Rather it has everything to do with our spiritual odour. Paul writes in Second Corinthians 2:

Now when I went to Troas to preach the gospel of Christ and found that the Lord had opened a door for me, I still had no peace of mind, because I did not find my brother Titus there. So I said good-bye to them and went on to Macedonia. But thanks be to God, who always leads us in triumphal procession in Christ and through us spreads everywhere the fragrance of the knowledge of him. For we are to God the aroma of Christ among those who are being saved and those who are perishing. To the one we are the smell of death; to the other, the fragrance of life. And who is equal to such a task? Unlike so many, we do not peddle the word of God for profit. On the contrary, in Christ we speak before God with sincerity, like men sent from God. 2Corinthians 2:12-17

Open doors usually encourage but Paul was discouraged despite this open door. If we look at two "open doors" in the New Testament, we might be tempted to consider an open door as a path that is cleared of obstacles:

Paul returns from the first of his missionary journeys to report how God had opened the door of faith to the Gentiles. Acts 14:27

Paul asks for prayer "that God may open a door for our message." Colossians 4:3

But, in First Corinthians 16, Paul explains why he has delayed a planned visit to Corinth. He writes:

"I will stay on at Ephesus until Pentecost, because a great door for effective work has opened to me, and there are many who oppose me." 1Corinthians 16:9

So an open door cannot always be considered as a path that is cleared of obstacles. It seems to me that an open door is a call of God to share the truth whether there are obstacles in the way or not.

In Second Corinthians 2, we find in verses 12 and 13 that Paul has gone to Troas and the Lord has opened a door of ministry for him there. But then in the next verse Paul writes that he had no peace of mind because he did not find Titus there. So he went on to Macedonia. Paul, like you and I, was human. He made mistakes in his personal life and I suspect that leaving Troas was one of them.

However, I want to make this point abundantly clear. When Paul was writing Scripture, he had the unique guidance and ministry of the inspiration of the Holy Spirit. That is why he could write the truth of God without human error.

Paul ignored the open door at Troas and moved on to find Titus. I suspect that a lack of faith gripped him in a weak moment and caused him to seek his own peace of mind over a ministry opportunity. At least he was honest about it. Paul makes no pretence of invincibility. He says in effect that he was so worried that he could not concentrate on ministry.

One vital part of any church that wants both to survive and to be used by God is the quality of its leadership. Who would prefer a leader who exudes an aura of strength to hide his weaknesses, to one who makes no attempt to conceal his weaknesses and who relies on God to use him despite his weaknesses?

What about us? Are we like Paul who was honest about his weaknesses? I discover a very encouraging truth in verse 14. God does not abandon us when we fail to walk through open doors. On the contrary, God keeps opening doors for us. He still leads us, guides and encourages us especially when He knows that our hearts are right towards Him. Paul found encouragement in the continual leading of a sovereign God. Despite Paul's problem and setback, he could still write in verse 14:

"...thanks be to God who always leads us" 2Corinthians 2:14

- We do not always follow
  But God is always willing to lead us.
- We do not always see the path clearly
  But God works all things after the counsel of His own will and for our good.

We usually see God's leading after events have occurred rather than during them but it is always there.

I will share my experience to illustrate the point. I had served as a pastor for many years when an invitation came along to head up Good News Broadcasting. I wrestled trying to discern God's Will. My wife and I loved the people in the church. Should we leave many years' worth of relationships? As has often happened, I had to make a decision without a clear understanding as to God's Will. But I can clearly see God's leading now.

Finding God's Will is not like aiming at a target and getting only God's second best if we miss the Bull's Eye.

Finding God's Will for us involves two considerations:

Our First and Primary Consideration:

We must be sure that our decisions are in keeping with God's Word.

Our Second Consideration:

We can then use the wisdom:

- That God has given us.
- Of the godly counsellors that God has provided to guide us and help us stay close to Him.

I believe that this is the way God leads His people and enables us to make wise decisions.

In verse 14, Paul refers to two ways that God leads us. Before we can understand the events that Paul is alluding to, we need to know some Roman history.

First: The Triumphal Processions

When the victorious Roman legions returned to Rome, the Emperor would reward the General by arranging a parade in his honour. The General would ride at the head of a long procession thronged by cheering crowds. Behind him came the regiments in their finest uniforms, their standards adorned with new battle honours. Then came wagons loaded with the spoils of war. Bringing up the rear were captured enemy soldiers in chains, destined for execution or slavery.

Second: The Fragrance of the Triumphal Processions

These processions could not only be heard and seen. They could also be smelled. Incense was burnt on either side of the processional route and the General and his regiments would make their way through clouds of incense with its fragrant odour.

Paul considered that the progress of the Gospel resembled a triumphal procession. He takes the long view because at any given time there may be as much in the ministry that looks like defeat as looks like victory.

But Paul knew that ultimately Christ would be victorious. He knew that he was participating as an ordinary foot-soldier in a parade that focused glory and honour on his Commander who led the procession.

Two Ways in Which God Leads Us

The First Way

God leads us to promised victory in Christ. Paul writes in verse 14:

"God always leads us in triumphal procession in Christ" 2Corinthians 2:14

The Second Way

God leads us to spread the fragrance of Christ. Paul continues in verse 14:

"God always leads us in triumphal procession in Christ and through us spreads everywhere the fragrance of the knowledge of him." 2Corinthians 2:14

Spreading the fragrance speaks of influence. We need to realise that everywhere we go we are influencing the world's attitude toward Christ. This is a solemn responsibility because we will only draw people to the Saviour if:

- Our lives are attractive.
- We care about people because they are created in the image of God.
- We are hard workers.
- We are responsible citizens.

- We will not draw people to the Saviour if we are obnoxious, selfish, greedy, negative or manipulative. Likewise, if people know that we claim to belong to Christ but behave as if we did not, we can do irreparable harm to His cause.

- Every day we are spreading the fragrance of the knowledge of Christ. However, it is towards God that the fragrance of our lives is primarily directed for we read in verse 15:

"For we are to God the aroma of Christ." 2Corinthians 2:15

Although we share the Gospel with people, in reality, God is our audience. Pleasing Him should be the passion of our lives. It was for Paul. Again and again he stresses that he is not a man-pleaser but a God-pleaser. In First Thessalonians 2 he states:

"We are not trying to please men but God, who tests our hearts. You know we never used flattery, nor did we put on a mask to cover up greed—God is our witness. We were not looking for praise from men, not from you or anyone else." 1Thessalonians 2:4-6

And in Galatians 1 Paul asks:

"Am I now trying to win the approval of men, or of God? Or am I trying to please men? If I were still trying to please men, I would not be a servant of Christ." Galatians 1:10

We must grasp these two essential truths:

- Our primary responsibility is to smell good to God.
- Men will want us to please them.

We could so easily get both distracted and discouraged if we do not keep our focus on God and what He wants from us. Paul expands the picture in verses 15 and 16:

"For we are to God the aroma of Christ among those who are being saved and those who are perishing. To the one we are the smell of death; to the other, the fragrance of life." 2Corinthians 2:15-16

To the soldiers and the jubilant spectators of the Roman victory procession, the smell of incense was associated with the heady excitement of success. However, to the prisoners of war bringing up the rear, the same scent had a vastly different significance because they faced execution or, at the best, slavery. What spoke of success and celebration to one group spoke of defeat and death to the other.

Paul is clearly stating three truths:

- We should not smell the same to everyone.

- We should smell like death to those who hate Christ and His truth.
- We should smell like life to those who see their need of a Saviour and respond.

I need to explore this further with you because sadly there are professing Christians who always smell the same and their smell is unpleasant. Let me explain:

- They are Christians but they smell like death to believer and unbeliever alike.

- Some Christians have unpleasant smells because of their demanding personalities, sour-puss attitudes, their legalism or laziness.

On the other hand you meet some Christians who are just sugary sweet with everyone and about everything. Despite their best efforts to smell pleasantly to everyone, they exude the wrong spiritual smell. Let me explain why:

- They do not preach anything but tolerance.
- They do not denounce sin, even when it hits them head-on, despite their obligation as God's people to stand for what is right and to oppose what is wrong.
- Their attitude exudes an aroma that offends no-one so that an agnostic, a humanist or a hedonist can enjoy their smell and fail to be challenged by:

  o The righteousness of God.
  o The message of The Gospel.
  o The demands of discipleship.

Note that Paul was willing to smell like death to some in order to be the fragrance of Christ to others.

In one church there were several women who were allergic to perfume. The church had to have a fragrance-free zone. Perfume produces a delightful fragrance for some but a sickening and potentially deadly fragrance for others. In the spiritual realm, the same is true. Some will be attracted to us. Others will react with disgust because they find Christ and His Gospel repugnant.

Let me sum-up what I have been teaching:

- If everyone hates us, there is probably a deficiency of love, grace or mercy in our lives.
- If everyone loves us, there is probably a deficiency of truth in our lives.
- There should be enough grace and mercy evident in our lives and actions that people whose hearts have been softened by the Holy Spirit will:

  - See the beauty of Christ in us.
  - Be attracted to Christ.
  - Respond to the Gospel when we speak to them.

- There should be enough bold truth emanating from our mouths that recoiling from us and even hating us will be those who have:

  - Been blinded by Satan to the truth of The Gospel.

97

○   Consciously chosen to live godless lives.

I would be the last one to tell you that this balance is easy to find or maintain. How often have we offended sincere seekers after truth with our poor representation of Christ? How often have we made God's enemies comfortable by smelling sweet when what they needed was bold truth? I know that it does not excuse us but Paul similarly struggled. I know this because he confesses to it in verse 16:

"And who is equal to such a task?" 2Corinthians 2:16

These words were written by Paul towards the end of his life. We should not therefore assume that the task gets easier the longer we are involved in communicating God's truth. Paul never ceased to find awe in his calling. To smell right to the right audience may actually be one of the most difficult tasks in the Christian life. The way we live our lives and the way we share our faith has tremendous consequences. The weight of lost souls is heavy and any thoughtful Christian will be asking the question that Paul asks:

"Who is equal to such a task?" 2Corinthians 2:16

In Second Corinthians 3:5 Paul answers this question. He states that by ourselves we are not competent but that:

"...our competence comes from God." 2Corinthians 3:5

Reverting back to Second Corinthians 2, we read in verse 17 that Paul writes how he responded to the task of spreading God's Word. He lets us know that there was a contrast between what he did and what many false teachers were doing. So we read:

"Unlike so many, we do not peddle the word of God for profit. On the contrary, in Christ we speak before God with sincerity, like men sent from God." 2Corinthians 2:17

The response of so many to the challenge of spreading the fragrance of Christ is to forget that:

- The ultimate task is to please God.
- God is our principal audience.
- The goal is to influence the lost for Christ.

Many regarded ministry as a business and as a way of getting rich. Paul refused to use his faith for financial gain. Look how he introduces this thought in verse 17:

"Unlike so many, we do not peddle the word of God for profit."

There were no money signs in Paul's ministry plans. Paul generally refused even to accept gifts for his services. Instead he chose to be bi-vocational in that he earned his own living expenses and those of his companions by making tents. By doing so, he offered the Gospel totally free. But Paul did not expect others to do that. That was his personal choice and he made it clear that it was proper for others to be paid. It is one thing to be paid, even well paid, for a job well done. It is quite another to peddle one's ministry for profit. This has been a common tragedy down through the centuries among the people of God.

Let us consider three examples in Scripture of greed getting the better of God's servants. We shall consider:

- Balaam the prophet.
- Gehazi, Elisha's servant.
- The spiritual shepherds of Israel in the days of Ezekiel.

- Balaam the Prophet

This prophet turned profiteer lived in the days of Israel's wandering in the desert. You can read his truly fascinating story in Numbers 22. Balaam was like some ministers. He said the right things about greed but not from his heart. Balak was the King of Moab. He asked Balaam to put a curse on the Israelites who were encamped nearby and appeared to be a threat. Balaam said he needed to consult with the Lord who told him in no uncertain terms not to do it. So Balaam declined Balak's request. Balak was not easily discouraged and offered to pay Balaam handsomely for a curse. Balaam answered him beautifully:

"Even if Balak gave me his palace filled with silver and gold, I could not do anything great or small to go beyond the command of the LORD my God." Numbers 22:18

Amazing! How can you beat that for commitment and obedience! But then Balaam made a fateful and almost fatal mistake by adding:

"Now stay here tonight as the others did and I will find out what *else* the LORD will tell me." Numbers 22:19

Balaam did not need to hear anything else from the Lord. God had already made His will perfectly well-known. I believe Balaam was trying to manipulate the situation in order to get money from Balak. So God sent an angel to take his life and he was spared only when his donkey balked in the road and subsequently lectured him.

- Gehazi, Elisha's Servant

Gehazi secretly requested payment from Naaman for Elisha's ministry to Naaman who was cured of leprosy. Do you know what God's judgment on Gehazi was? Gehazi became a leper.

- The Spiritual Shepherds of Israel

We read in Ezekiel 34 that the Lord sent Ezekiel to denounce them:

'This is what the Sovereign LORD says: Woe to the shepherds of Israel who only take care of themselves! Should not shepherds take care of the flock? You eat the curds, clothe yourselves with the wool and slaughter the choice animals, but you do not take care of the flock." Ezekiel 34:2

Even today or perhaps I should say especially today it is common for pastors to hear the call of God when a larger church that offers a bigger salary has a vacancy. It is not unusual for mega-church pastors to accept a lot of money in book sales for books written in church time.

And the temptation to greed is not just affecting pastors. When I was a pastor, the church would be contacted by well-known Christian artistes and others who wanted to come to the church to assist us in our outreach and other ministries and to be paid a lot of money for the privilege of doing so.

I well understand the need to live as I have to as much as anyone else. I want to make this clear. I am not saying that it is wrong for God's servants to be paid for their services. What I am saying is this. Ministry should never be for sale or profit and Paul's certainly was not.

Paul's preaching was always Christ-centred. I cannot overstress the importance of this. In verse 17 he writes:

"On the contrary, in Christ we speak before God with sincerity, like men sent from God." 2Corinthians 2:17

Paul spoke in Christ. It meant that for Paul:

- Christ was his chief Subject.
- Christ was his chief Object.
- Christ was his chief Motivator.

Paul spoke before God as one sent from God. He was always aware that he was only an ambassador, that is, one who speaks for another without any message or authority of his own. Paul was aware of his solemn responsibility to convey his Master's message. So he spoke:

- Accurately.
- Faithfully.
- Completely.

And Paul spoke with sincerity. What did he not do in order to obtain a favourable response or to gain financially? He did not:

- Change his words to accommodate his hearers
- Adapt his words to the reactions of his hearers.
- Conceal his true motives.
- Pervert the truth.

I want to conclude by reminding you of the important point that we read about in verse 17 that I trust will help you as you seek to spread the fragrance of the knowledge of Christ.

Paul's preaching was always Christ-centred:

Christ was his chief Subject.

Christ was his chief Object.

Christ was his chief Motivator.

Chapter 6

How To Be Holy

If you phone Good News Broadcasting outside of office hours you will be connected to an answering machine with a recording that thanks you for calling and asks you to leave a message. However, many calls are received when the offices are closed but without a message. We understand the problem. We all like the personal touch.

I have a list of messages that were recorded on answering machines. Three that made me smile were:

- Hi! John's answering machine is broken. This is his refrigerator. Please speak slowly and I'll stick your message to me with one of those little magnets.

- Greetings, you have reached the Extra Sensory Perception research department. We know who you are and what you want, so, at the sound of the tone, please hang up.

- Hello, I'm not answering the phone. I'm trying to avoid an obnoxious person. Leave a message, and if I don't call you back, you'll know it's you.

If you could call God's answering machine, what would you hear? I think you might hear something like this:

"You shall be holy, for I the Lord, your God am holy."

I say that because that important message is repeated several times in Scripture. For example, in First Peter 1, Peter has been laying a foundation about the meaning of salvation and from verse 13 he builds upon it the concept of holiness.

"Therefore, prepare your minds for action; be self-controlled; set your hope fully on the grace to be given you when Jesus Christ is revealed. As obedient children, do not conform to the evil desires you had when you lived in ignorance. But just as he who called you is holy, so be holy in all you do; for it is written: "Be holy, because I am holy." Since you call on a Father who judges each man's work impartially, live your lives as strangers here in reverent fear." 1Peter 1:13-17

The word "holy" is one of the most common words in the Bible and yet it is one of the most misunderstood words in our English language. People use the word "holy". Have you ever heard anyone say, "Holy Smoke?"

Some might recall the Batman stories and remember that Batman's sidekick Robin used that expression every time he was surprised.

God has called us to be holy but how many of you would want that word on your résumé? How would you react if, when describing you, I said, "They are kind, friendly, funny, loving, compassionate...and holy?" The first group of descriptive words has a favourable impact on people but not everyone feels at ease about the last description "holy." A lot of people would immediately think of "a holy Joe" and people use those words derisively when they mock and scoff at Christians.

We also hear the word "holy" applied to people who have chosen a simple way of life that is so totally different from the life styles of the vast majority. Such people are often regarded as "holy" even if their personal beliefs and any cult or sect that they belong to deny the existence of God or their chosen life style is simply their way of getting away from "the rat race" or saving the planet. Whilst such people may well be sincere in the way they choose to live, sincerity is not holiness and their conduct has nothing to do with biblical holiness.

In this chapter we will examine the wonderful concept of biblical holiness from two perspectives:

- God's Holiness.

- Our Holiness.

God Is Holy

There are many Bible words that describe the character and nature of God. So we can, for example, read that God is:

- Spirit.
- Light.
- Love.
- Jehovah-Jireh, our Provider
- El Shaddai, the Almighty One.

There are many more words and titles used to describe the richness and beauty of God's Character. But there is one description that appears more than any other:

God is HOLY

In Isaiah 6, we read that Isaiah had a vision of the Lord high and lifted up. In the vision, the seraphim hovering above God were shouting to each other:

"Holy, holy, holy is the Lord God Almighty; the whole earth is full of his glory!" Isaiah 6:3

In the Bible, we often find that the word "holy" is repeated three times when it refers to God. In Jewish thinking, three was a divine number. We recognise the significance - Father, Son and Holy Spirit. So the seraphim do not shout, "Holy" or "Holy, holy." They shout, "Holy, holy, holy!" What does the word 'holy' mean?

The Hebrew word used in the Old Testament means:

- To cut apart or to separate.

In the New Testament the word used is the word for sanctified or consecrated. It means:

- Separate, distinct or different."

So, for a working definition, holy means:

- Set apart or different.

Let me give you two examples:

- I have a Holy Bible. The word biblos means "book." When we say it is the Holy Bible we are saying it is different from any other book ever written. It is the only book written by God.
- The Temple in Jerusalem was called the "Holy Temple." It was the only building used for the worship of the true and living God.

So, when we say God is holy, we are saying that God is unique. He is the ONE–and nobody else is like Him.

The Psalmist says about God:

"In the council of the holy ones God is greatly feared; he is more awesome than all who surround him. O Lord God Almighty, who is like you? You are mighty, O Lord, and your faithfulness surrounds you." Psalm 89:7

In heaven, John saw heavenly creatures praising God and John recorded that:

"Day and night they never stop saying, 'Holy, holy, holy is the Lord God Almighty, who was, and is, and is to come!'" Revelation 4:8

We Are To Be Holy

In First Peter 1, Peter gives us some practical advice on how to reflect God's holiness in our lives. Peter does not just say, "Be holy" and then leave it up to us to figure out how to be holy but starting in verse 13 he gives us five areas of our lives where holiness operates:

- First: Holiness involves OUR MINDS.

- Second: Holiness involves OUR WILLS.

- Third: Holiness involves OUR FUTURES.

- Fourth: Holiness involves OUR CONDUCT.

- Fifth: Holiness involves OUR JUDGEMENT.

First: Holiness involves OUR MINDS

Peter writes in verse 13:

"...prepare your minds for action." 1Peter 1:13 (NIV)

Being holy begins with the right attitude. You must decide you will be holy. The Authorised Version or King James translation of this verse says:

"...gird up the loins of your mind." 1Peter 1:13 (AV)

Back in Bible times men wore long flowing robes. When they wanted to run, they picked up the hem of their robes and tucked it into their belts. That was called "girding up your loins." In other words, you have got to desire to be holy and that begins in your mind. Peter is literally writing:

"Get ready to be holy."

Houdini, the great illusionist and escape artist, was in tremendous physical condition. He bragged that he could withstand any blow to his abdomen without flinching. He was challenged by a man but Houdini was distracted and did not have time to prepare for the punch. He died from a ruptured appendix. In a real sense that is exactly what Peter means because we need to prepare ourselves mentally for the attacks of the world, the flesh and the devil. If we are not in the right frame of mind, we will suffer a 'sucker punch' from our spiritual enemies.

Sadly, too many people hunger for happiness rather than holiness. A.W. Tozer wrote:

"The emphasis of the New Testament is not upon happiness but holiness. God is more concerned with the state of people's hearts than with the state of their feelings. Go to God and tell Him that it is your desire to be holy at any cost and then ask Him to make you holy whether you are happy or not. Be assured that in the end you will be as happy as you are holy; but for the time being let your whole ambition be to serve God and be Christ-like." A.W. Tozer

Second: Holiness involves OUR WILLS

Peter writes in verse 13:

"Be-self controlled." 1Peter 1:13

Being holy demands our determination to succeed.

I love the story of the father who, though sceptical of his teenage son's new found determination to build bulging muscles, followed him to the weight-lifting department. They admired a set of weights. "Please," pleaded the teenager. "I promise I'll use them every day.""I don't know, Michael. It's really a big commitment on your part and they're not cheap either," the father said. "I'll use them, Dad, I promise, you'll see." Finally won over, the father paid for the equipment and headed for the door. After a few steps, he heard his son behind him say, "What! You mean I've got to carry them all the way to the car park?"

That story reminds me somewhat of some people's commitment to follow Christ. It is theory rather than practice. It is in our attitudes but not our actions. Your will is what causes you to get out of a warm bed on a cold morning, get dressed, drive to a church building, and find a parking place so that you can worship and study the Bible. You make a decision with your mind but it is your will that makes it happen.

Peter is writing about the need to exercise self-control when you are tempted to sin. It is your will that says "No" when you are tempted to sin. But resisting temptation is often much harder than simply saying, "No." We all have an external source of temptation. He is the devil. But we also have an internal source of temptation that the Bible refers to as "the flesh" or "self." It is the big "I" that says, "Go ahead, if it feels good, do it!" This "self" must be crucified. The voice of "self" must always be silenced or it will lead us into sin.

Each of us has a control centre in our lives. It is like a throne. Whoever sits on the throne controls our lives. Let me illustrate it with a description, which is taken from Campus Crusade Ministries, of two circles.

The First Circle: King Self is on the throne. Christ is present in the believer's life but He is not allowed to control it. As a result, all the believer's other interests are unbalanced and that produces frustration. Does this circle represent your life? Is self controlling you?

The Second Circle: This represents God's will for our lives. We enthrone King Jesus as Lord of our life. To do this we dethrone King Self and yield ourselves to Jesus. When we do, all other interests are in balance which produces harmony and blessing for us. That is what it means to exercise self-control and it is part of being holy. Self-control is one of the fruits of the Spirit. So, as you surrender your life to the power of the Holy Spirit dwelling within you, your self-control will increase.

Third: Holiness involves OUR FUTURES

Peter writes in verse 13:

"Set your hope fully on the grace to be given you when Jesus Christ is revealed." 1Peter 1:13

Being holy includes expecting the return of our Saviour, Jesus Christ. That phrase 'Set your hope fully' means to "completely establish your hope." The source of our hope is the return of Jesus Christ. Paul wrote about this:

"Looking for that blessed hope, and the glorious appearing of our great God and Saviour, Jesus Christ." Titus 2:13

Sometimes Hollywood produces a film with a message and the 1994 film, "The Shawshank Redemption," is a story about hope. It is set in the 1940s and it is about a banker named Andy who is wrongly convicted of killing his wife and sent to prison for two life terms. In prison he is befriended by a prisoner named Red who has been in prison for so long that he has lost hope. Every time Red appears before the Parole Board, he does not expect to be released and he is not. His hopelessness grows. Andy is a man full of determination and hope and he plants the seeds of hope in his friend. He tells him about a certain place where there is a container buried in a stone wall beside a cornfield at the base of a large tree. He tells him that this container holds a great treasure. This awakens a sense of hope in Red. He begins to believe there is something valuable outside the world of the prison and it is worth living for. His hope sustains him and on his release he finds the promised treasure. What a great lesson about hope!

There is a treasure waiting for all of us when we are released from this life. He was once buried treasure but He became resurrected treasure! His name is Jesus and just knowing that you will see His face should give you enough hope to endure anything this life has to throw at you. Set your hope firmly on Jesus.

Fourth: Holiness involves OUR CONDUCT

Peter writes in verse 14:

"As obedient children, do not conform to the evil desires you had when you lived in ignorance." 1Peter 1:14

Being holy means that you dare to be different but holiness has nothing to do with your hairstyle or the clothes you wear. Holiness involves behaving differently from the people who are not followers of Jesus Christ. But despite this good difference between those who follow Jesus and those who do not, the media loves to ridicule anything that is Christian. Committed Christians are mocked and portrayed as religious fanatics. Why? Because they chose to be different. They chose to be holy. No such derision is reserved for those unusual religious oddballs who live weird lives and make claims that they can hear voices directing them and the like. They are portrayed by the media as "holy people" and in consequence the general public also regard them as holy. Hence, when we speak about holiness, many unbelievers do not want to be holy. Unlike us, unbelievers do not appreciate that being holy makes you different but it does not make you weird. Being holy means living such a God-filled life of kindness and gentleness that your life becomes attractive to others.

Consider the lifestyle of Jesus, the most holy man who ever lived. Jesus mixed with the social outcasts of His day. He spoke to the traitorous and dishonest Jewish tax collectors who worked for the Romans, the prostitutes and the drunkards. He spoke to the lepers who warned everyone to stay away from them with their shouts of

"Unclean, unclean." Jesus wanted to give these outcasts the opportunity to have a new life if they would repent and believe the Gospel.

Jesus told simple stories that could make people laugh as He explained divine truth in such a way that ordinary people could understand what God required of them. He was without sin and He never compromised His Divine nature. He had the kind of personality that made Him attractive. In his Gospel Mark writes:

"...the common people heard him gladly." Mark 12:37

The only people who did not like Jesus were the pompous religious leaders. They were more interested in their external and artificial self-righteousness that gave other people the false impression that they were holy men.

We are not to give in to the evil desires that are so prevalent today. But what about those desires that are now so commonplace that they almost escape being regarded as evil? Let me ask two questions. Have these sins been reclassified and are they now acceptable?

- Gluttony.
- Greed.
- Meanness.
- Selfishness.

116

How many times do you hear the slang expression "Gimme," that is often used as a shorter version of, "I want something now and I don't care about anybody else but me!"

When we hear stories about the indifference shown toward people, it is so very easy for us to say "Oh, if I'd been there, I would have taken time to help." Yet we know that there are hurting and lonely people all around us. So do we care about them? Caring about them, showing kindness to strangers, is what it means to be holy. God says, "I am the Lord God and I am Different, so you be Different too!"

Fifth: Holiness involves OUR JUDGEMENT

Peter writes in verse 17:
"Since you call on a Father who judges each man's work impartially, live your lives as strangers here in reverent fear." 1Peter 1:17

Being holy demands a respectful fear of God. Peter speaks of God as our Father. When I was growing up I respected my father. I knew that if I broke his rules punishment would follow. But I never cringed in fear of him. To live in fear of God does not mean that we cringe in fear and turn away from Him. It means that we have a holy awe and respect for Him. I am amazed at how many people do not live in fear of the Living God.

We need to be holy because one day we will be judged. One day, God is going to judge us impartially. As Christians, we will not be judged to determine whether we go to hell or heaven. That has already been settled. This judgment is when God examines what we did with what He gave us. Each of us who are followers of Jesus will be called upon to give an account for how we lived our Christian lives and this should motivate all of us to be holy.

A little girl on the way home from church, turned to her mother and said, "Mummy, the preacher's sermon this morning confused me."The mother said, "Oh! Why is that? "The girl replied, "Well, he said that God is bigger than we are. Is that true?" "Yes, that's true," the mother replied. "He also said that God lives within us. Is that true too?" The mother replied, "Yes." "Well," said the girl. "If God is bigger than us and He lives in us wouldn't He show through?"

I like that little girl's way of putting it. If God lives in us, then there is no way of keeping Him from "showing through." That is the essence of Christian living. We must live in such a way that people around see God in our lives.

Chapter 7

How To Manage Temptation

The Lord of the Rings trilogy tell a fascinating story. These three films portray the friendship of Frodo Baggins and Sam Gamgee. Now, in case some of you have not seen the movies or read the books let me tell you more. The central character, a halfling or hobbit named Frodo, has the responsibility of destroying a powerful and inherently evil ring. The only way this can be done is by travelling hundreds of miles across enemy-held territory called Mordor to throw the ring into the volcano where it was originally forged by the evil Sauron, a sort of a satan-like character. This involves a long and perilous journey. At one point Frodo decides to strike out on his own so as not to endanger any of the other members of the fellowship who had also set out to help him with this task. But his friend Sam will hear nothing of Frodo going it alone and it was a good thing that he decided to let faithful Sam accompany him because there are several times when he would not have made it if it were not for him.

This story puts a spotlight on the fact that we all need friends. Life in this sinful world can be hard and we were not designed to go through it alone. God did not make us self-sufficient beings. We see this in the very beginning of human history. When God made Adam, He saw that it was not good for him to be without a companion so He made Eve.

This should remind us that we were made to live our lives with others. We need friends. And I am sure you will agree that true friends, friends like Sam, who "stick closer than a brother" no matter what life brings, are precious. Perhaps this thought inspired this poem:

"Count your garden by the FLOWERS
Never by the LEAVES that fall
Count your days by golden HOURS
Do not remember the CLOUDS at all.
Count your nights by STARS, not SHADOWS.
Count your life with SMILES, not TEARS.
And with joy on every birthday,
Count your age by FRIENDS not YEARS"

The relationship between Sam and Frodo illustrates the truth that one of the benefits of having friends is that we can talk to them when life gets tough. Sam and Frodo have some wonderful conversations. They give each other counsel that helps them succeed in completing their difficult task. That is the way it should be between good friends. Proverbs 27 says:

"...the pleasantness of one's friend springs from his EARNEST COUNSEL." Proverbs 27: 9

When we have a dilemma one of the first things we do is to go to our friends for their input. I want to be like a friend to you as I take God's Word and apply it to the subject of temptation. There are two passages of Scripture which will help us. The first is in First Corinthians 10 and the second is in James 1.

So, if you think you are standing firm, be careful that you don't fall! No temptation has seized you except what is common to man. And God is faithful; he will not let you be tempted beyond what you can bear. But when you are tempted, he will also provide a way out so that you can stand up under it. 1Corinthians 10:12-14

When tempted, no-one should say, "God is tempting me." For God cannot be tempted by evil, nor does he tempt anyone; but each one is tempted when, by his own evil desire, he is dragged away and enticed. Then, after desire has conceived, it gives birth to sin; and sin, when it is full-grown, gives birth to death. James 1:13-15

If I said that everyone struggles with temptation, would you agree or do you think that some are exempt from temptation and:

- Can stand firm despite temptation?
- Are beyond the reach of temptation?

1 Corinthians 10:13 warns all of us that we should be careful because temptation is "common to man." No

one is immune to the problem. Being tempted is part of being human. It follows that:

- It is inevitable that all of us will be enticed or tempted to do wrong from time to time.
- The temptations that we face will have been faced by others.
- When others tell us that they are being tempted, we must tell them that there is nothing abnormally wrong with them.

Perhaps you have seen the car sticker that says, "Lead me not into temptation; I am perfectly capable of finding it on my own." Well, that humorously sets out the truth that in life all people find themselves face to face with temptation. Even mature Christians, believers who make it their goal to walk as close to God as they possibly can, wrestle with temptation every single day. Like the rain, temptation falls on the just and the unjust. C. S. Lewis once said:

"A silly idea is current that good people do not know what temptation means. This is an obvious lie. Only those who try to resist temptation know how strong it is."

The fact is that all of us are sinful fallen creatures so all of us are tempted. The monk who lives behind cloistered walls wrestles with temptation just as much as the salesman out on the road.

It is not a sin to be tempted

Jesus Himself experienced temptation and He therefore knows how temptation affects us. We read in Hebrews: "For we do not have a High Priest who is unable to sympathise with our weaknesses, but we have One who has been tempted in every way, just as we are—yet without sin." Hebrews 4:15

So, we do not sin at the time we are being tempted but we do sin the moment that we:

- Yield to temptation.
- Act on our evil thoughts and selfish desires.

Temptations come in all shapes and sizes.

Some think that temptations are limited to sexual sins but that is not true. There are all kinds of temptation. Some are tempted to:

- Take revenge.
- Win at all costs.
- Be envious or jealous.
- Hate or be violent.

But these are just a few of the range of temptations that we all wrestle with. Let us do a quick test to illustrate this. Have you ever been tempted to:

- Eat or spend too much?
- Hold a grudge?
- Lie or to call in sick when you were not?
- Drive faster than the speed limit?
- Sin sexually?

If we were at a party and these questions were part of a compulsory quiz that everyone had to answer honestly by a show of hands, we would see everyone's hands raised and lowered at some time during the quiz because the truth is all of us are tempted in a wide variety of ways each and every day.

ALL Temptation is from SATAN

This is important for us to know because if we are to win our battle with temptation we have to understand what or rather WHO we are up against. The dictionary defines temptation as:

"The act of enticement to do wrong by the promise of pleasure or gain."

I consider that to be a good working definition because temptation tries to motivate us to be bad by promising something that is good. That sound just like the devil's tactics to me. Ephesians reminds us that when it comes to temptation:

"... our struggle is not just against flesh and blood. It is against the powers of this dark world—the spiritual forces of evil." Ephesians 6:12

So, as this text and numerous others like it indicate, our temptations are orchestrated by the powers of darkness. You see, the truth is there is an evil force at work in this world. That force is controlled by the devil, or to refer to him by his name as Jesus did, Satan, and it is Satan who seeks to destroy our lives. One of the ways that Satan seeks to do this is by stirring up our desires.

Satan hopes that we will:

- Respond to our desires in sinful ways.
- Take the wrong path and pay the painful consequences.

Satan does these things because he wants to:

- Ruin our lives.
- Demolish our Christian witness.

In John's Gospel Jesus describes Satan as a thief but a thief who acts differently from other thieves. What does Satan do? Satan comes not only to steal but to kill and destroy. Jesus said:

"The thief's purpose is to steal and kill and destroy. My purpose is to give them a rich and satisfying life." John 10:10

Satan's intentions regarding us:

- Satan wants to steal the joy that God intends you and me to have in life.
- Satan wants to destroy us.

Today many people, even some Christians, tend to downplay a belief in a literal devil. If you are one of them, then let me ask you how you to explain these evils that are just a few of the many worldwide problems that I could mention:

- The slaughter in warfare of so many millions, mostly over border disputes and ethnic differences and the problem still exists.
- The existence of worldwide racial prejudice and hatred and so-called religious wars.
- The starvation of millions of children. They still starved to death today and yet across the borders from where they die there is enough food even for house pets.
- The nauseating sexual abuse of children, some by their own parents.

Explain these moral insanities. Are they caused by:

- A damaged chromosome here and there?
- Poverty and poor housing conditions?
- An ineffective education system?
- A lack of parental discipline?

Come on! It is so much deeper than that:

- It is evil.
- It is organised evil.
- There is intentionality behind it.

So James writes in his letter:

"We must not be deceived..." James 1:16

There is a force at work in this world and in your life and mine. It is the force of evil and its leader is a fallen angel named Satan. He wants to wreck your life and one way he does it is by stirring up the dark destructive desires that dwell in each of us. These desires, if we let them, will destroy us.

So when we or others need guidance about temptation, we must understand that temptation is inevitable. But when we yield to it, it is our fault. James writes:

"Each one is tempted when he is carried away and enticed by his own lust." James 1:14

Draw a line under the words, "each one" and "own" to remind you that when we choose to give in to temptation and we sin, we cannot blame anyone else. Each one of us is responsible for what we say and do. "The devil made me do it," and similar excuses, are lies.

The fact is that nothing outside ourselves is strong enough, not even Satan, to cause us to sin.

Satan is a powerful enemy but he is a defeated enemy, so we cannot blame him for our sin. No, sin takes place when we agree to his temptations and of our own free will decide to follow them. In other words, no one has to yield to temptation. No one has to cross the line and sin. We have a choice. Anyone who says, "I cannot help myself" is lying and deluding themselves. Let me give you an example to show you how true this principle is.

Let us suppose you are at home alone and you decide to yield to temptation and watch a pornographic movie. I know that is an extreme example but stay with me. You tune in to the appropriate "adult" channel and start to watch but a few minutes into the film you hear a car on your driveway and a car door open and close. You look out the window and you see me about to knock on your door. Could you stop watching the movie? Of course you could, because no sin is irresistible.

We do not have to lose the battle with temptation. We can say no. In fact, God promises that He will never allow us to be tempted beyond what we can bear. God is our Creator, our Designer. He knows our limits and He has promised that He will not allow Satan to exert more pressure on us than we can say "no" to.

Years ago many ships sank because they were carrying too much cargo and were too low in the water. Well, after decades of tragic losses, a man in England by the name of Plimsoll came up with the idea that a line should be painted on the side of merchant vessels, so that it would be easy to tell if they were too low in the water. This became known as the "Plimsoll Line." It became illegal for ships to be loaded beyond the Plimsoll Line and in the same way, there is a "Plimsoll Line" on our lives. God will not allow Satan to tempt us beyond what we are able to handle. God will not let Satan overload us with more enticements than we can carry. This is what Paul writes in First Corinthians 10 verse 13. God:

"... will always provide us with a way out." 1Corinthians 10:13

Some translations word it this way:

"When you are tempted God will also provide a way of ESCAPE..." ICorinthians 10:13

I want to take that word "ESCAPE" and use it as an acronym to help us remember six vital truths that we must know or do to win this war against temptation.

The way to E.S.C.A.P.E from temptation

E: Environment
S: Spend time with God
C: Claim Scripture

A: Accountability
P: Pleasure and Pain
E: Evangelism

The First Vital Truth is: Environment

One obvious way of avoiding temptation altogether is to stay away from environments where temptations exist. Paul in Ephesians alludes to this principle when he writes:

"See then that you walk CIRCUMSPECTLY, not as fools, but as wise." Ephesians 5:15

In other words we should walk AROUND places where we know temptation waits to entice us. And as this verse says, it is foolish to go where you know the devil is lying in wait ready and willing to tempt you. We would all be better off today if Adam and Eve had steered clear of that forbidden tree in the Garden of Eden. Satan still waits in forbidden places, places that God wants us to stay away from and this is why Paul warns us to walk circumspectly. The book of Proverbs also warns us:

"Do not set your foot on the path of the wicked" Proverbs 4:14

This is another way of saying that not only should we avoid places where we are tempted, we should also steer clear of paths of the wicked that lead to places where this will happen. We must do everything we can to avoid anything that can lead us to sin.

I read about a Christian who does not wear sunglasses when he goes to the beach because they make it too easy for him to look where he should not be looking without his wife or Christian friends knowing the direction of his glances. He is a wise man. He knows what it means to walk circumspectly. Sunglasses can be helpful, even necessary, but I take his point. We should follow his example and keep out of environments where we know we might be tempted to sin.

If you have a problem with:

- Gossip: stay away from people who cannot keep their noses out of other people's business.
- Eating too much: do not buy your coffee at a donut shop.
- Alcohol: do not eat your meals in bars.

In short, stay away from people, places and things that you know could cause you to stumble. Remember, it is easier to stay out of temptation than to get out of temptation.

When we foolishly spend time near people, places or things that we know will tempt us, we are playing right into the hands of Satan. This is what Paul was getting at in Romans. He wrote:

"Do not go on presenting the members of your body to sin." Romans 6:13

The Second Vital Truth is: Spend time with God

One of the greatest weapons in this war that we all wage with temptation is to keep a daily appointment with our Almighty, all-loving God.

I say this because the closer we get to God the more clearly we see Satan for who he really is. We need to have our spiritual eyes opened and we will only achieve this as we:

- Spend time with God.
- Learn His perspective on our lives.
- Learn to think His thoughts.

The deeper our relationship with God is, the better we can see through the Satan's lies and understand the potential consequences of our sin. The more time we spend with God the easier it is for us to say 'no' to Satan's invitations and inducements.

When Jesus was tempted in the desert for forty days He said to Satan:

"Away from Me! For it is written 'Worship the Lord your God and serve Him only." Matthew 4:10

Jesus was essentially saying to Satan that He wanted Satan to leave Him alone because He belonged to God. We too belong to God and not to Satan. We need to have a deep relationship with God so that we can say to Satan, with absolute confidence and assurance, what Jesus said to him.

We also come to see that temptation can be good for us because it gives us an opportunity for us to grow closer to God by obeying Him instead of yielding to Satan.

The Third Vital Truth is: Claim Scripture

The Gospels record that Jesus' primary weapon when He faced temptation was Scripture. Three times Satan tempted Jesus. On each occasion Jesus responded by saying:

"It is written..." Matthew 4:1-11

This should remind us that the Bible is one of our weapons in our wars with Satan and temptation. When Paul was writing to the Ephesians, he calls Satan "the evil one" and he refers the Word of God, the Bible, as "the sword of the Spirit." Paul wrote:

"...take up the shield of faith, with which you can extinguish all the flaming arrows of the evil one. Take the helmet of salvation and the sword of the Spirit, which is the word of God. Ephesians 6:16-17

David, unlike us, did not have the benefit of the New Testament but he understood that the Scriptures were God's Word. He also understood the principle that if we have God's Word in our hearts, we have a weapon that will defend us against sin. In Psalm 119 he wrote:

"How can a young man keep his way pure? By living according to Your Word...I have hidden Your Word in my heart that I might not sin against You." Psalm 119: 9

I know this must seem obvious but the truth of it is so important that it must be worth stating. You cannot hide in your heart something that you have not got. So, the more Scripture you learn, the more Scripture you can "hide in your heart" so that you can use it when you are under attack. The more we learn the more:

- Knowledgeable we will become about sin.
- Knowledgeable we will become about Satan.
- Easily we will handle the Sword of the Spirit.
- Power we will experience over temptation.

It is as though every verse we "put into our hearts" becomes an anti-missile that we can fire to shoot down the projectiles Satan launches against us.

Let me show you some examples:

- When you first feel drawn to sin you can fire off: "Submit yourselves to God. Resist the devil and he will flee from you." James 4:7.
- When tempted to lie or cheat, you could use: "The Lord abhors dishonest scales but accurate weights are His delight." Proverbs 11:1.

- When you are tired and tempted to take a verbal shot at one of your kids, you can rely on:
"...do not provoke your children." Ephesians 6:4.

That is how the Bible works. When it is stored up in our hearts, it stands ready to strike automatically and no weapon can stand against the truth of Scripture.

God often provides a way of escape through the power of His Word. Dwight Moody wisely said about the Bible:

"Sin will keep you from this Book and this book will keep you from sin." Dwight Moody.

The Fourth Vital Truth is: Accountability

I am using this word to refer to the good practice of using a Christian friend to be your accountability partner. You mention a problem to the friend and ask for their help. Do not confuse this practice with the disclosure of sin. Let me give you two examples to illustrate the difference:

- First example: Disclosure occurs if you tell your friend that you watch porn on the internet. Accountability is asking your friend to keep the computer until you can overcome the problem.
- Second example: Disclosure is telling your friend that you are arguing with your parents and being unkind to them. Accountability is having them call

your parents once a week to see how you are behaving.

Accountability is a good thing because Christian friends can give us a lot of power when it comes to saying "no" to temptation. This story will prove my point.

There was a horse pull in Canada where one horse pulled 9,000 pounds and another 8,000 pounds. When teamed together you would expect them to pull 17,000 pounds. Not so! Together, they could pull 30,000 pounds! This principle is called synergism. It means the working together of two things to produce an effect greater than the sum of their individual effects. We all know that much more can be done in a team effort than can be accomplished solo and that is the way it is with temptation.

The Fifth Vital Truth is: Pleasure and Pain

I would be foolish as would anyone who denied that sin was pleasurable. But, the pleasures that come with yielding to temptation and sinning are temporary whereas the pain that always follows goes on and on. Moses understood this. In Hebrews it says about Moses that:

"...he...refused to be known as the son of Pharaoh's daughter. He chose to be mistreated along with the people of God rather than to enjoy the pleasures of sin for a short time." Hebrews 11:24-25

136

I have heard mature believers say that whenever they are tempted by sexual sin, they find it helpful to review the painful effects that such actions have:

- One day looking Jesus in the face and having to give an account.
- Inflicting untold hurt on my loyal wife and losing her respect and trust.
- Hurting my beloved daughters.
- Destroying my example and credibility with my children. Nullifying both present and future efforts to teach them to obey God.
- Causing shame to my family.

Whenever we are tempted to sin, we should ask God to open our eyes so that we can see all the pain our sin will cause. This can be a powerful motivation to say "no" to Satan's invitations.

The Sixth Vital Truth is: Evangelism

When we yield to temptation and sin, we lose something very precious, the power of our personal witness. Many non-believers are looking for an excuse not to take the claims of Christ seriously and often all it takes is for them to see us involved in sinful behaviour.

We often talk about how wonderful it will be in heaven when people tell us that something we did or said led them to faith in Jesus. But can you imagine the reverse? Can you imagine how painful it would be for us to walk the streets of Hell and have people tell us that they would have become Christians but for our behaviour? They saw us sin and concluded that our faith in Jesus was just an empty sham. They are in Hell because of what we did. How would we answer them?

In the last paragraph I asked you to use your imagination because I want to make it quite clear that Christians will not walk the streets of Hell. But they will stand before God's Throne. When they do, I do think that they will have an understanding of their sin. In the light of God's holiness they will, for the first time, comprehend the true depth of their sinfulness. Perhaps this is why the Bible says that God will "wipe tears from our eyes..." Maybe they are the tears that we will shed when we realise that our sins kept others from trusting in Jesus. Do you know of any sin that is so pleasurable that it is worth that pain?

One of the wonderful things about Christian fellowship is that because we recognise that we are only sinners saved by the grace of God, we can be honest and help one another with each other's struggles, temptations and failures.

Chapter 8

How To Grow Up

Have you ever said to someone, "Will you grow up?" Maybe you say something like, "Will you act your age and not your shoe size?" It is the same message and usually said to an adult who is acting childishly. In total contrast, Jesus said these words to adults about their need to repent:

"I tell you the truth, unless you change and become like little children, you will never enter the kingdom of heaven." Matthew 18:3

Little children possess the remarkable ability to express wonder and trust and we need to reclaim these in our relationship with God. But there is a great difference between being child-like and being childish. Children also have the tendency to be selfish and pout. They are messy, too. A man and his wife put their children to bed and on returning to the lounge they could hardly walk for all the toys on the floor. As they were picking the toys up the man turned to his wife and said in a weary voice, "I finally understand the Scripture that says, 'when I became a man, I put away childish things!'"

As you know, Paul was not referring to toys when he wrote verse 11 of First Corinthians 13, he was writing about spiritual maturity. Sadly, there are some who never seem to grow up. They just grow older.

In his First Epistle, Peter concludes Chapter 1 and commences Chapter 2 with these five verses:

For "All men are like grass, and all their glory is like the flowers of the field; the grass withers and the flowers fall, but the word of the Lord stands for ever." And this is the word that was preached to you. 1Peter 1:24-25

Therefore, rid yourselves of all malice and all deceit, hypocrisy, envy, and slander of every kind. Like newborn babies, crave pure spiritual milk, so that by it you may grow up in your salvation, now that you have tasted that the Lord is good. 1Peter 2:1-3

Peter contrasts the shortness and frailty of human life with the eternal Word of the Lord which we have been taught. In the light of this, Peter challenges his readers to grow up spiritually.

I believe that a major problem today is that there are thousands of immature Christians who should be growing. There are many adults who have known the Lord for many years but they are spiritual babies because they have never grown in their salvation. They are self-centred, mean and envious.

If you are interested in growing up in your salvation, Peter's words are worth serious consideration and he indicates three principles that deal with spiritual growth. They are:
- Keeping rubbish in your life stunts your growth.
- A desire for God's Word stimulates your growth.
- Friendship with Jesus as Lord supports your growth

Keeping rubbish in your life stunts your growth

"Therefore, rid yourselves of all malice and all deceit, hypocrisy, envy, and slander of every kind." 1Peter 2:1

Peter identifies four specific things that will stunt our spiritual growth and that we need to get rid of. The Greek word translated "rid yourselves" is used to describe someone taking off a filthy garment. For instance, in John 11 we read the amazing story of how Jesus raised Lazarus when he had been dead for four days. They opened the tomb and Jesus called, "Lazarus, come out!" Lazarus stumbled out because he had strips of cloth binding both his hands and his feet and covering his face. Jesus said, "Take off the grave clothes and let him go!"

Lazarus had life but he was restricted by those stinking grave clothes. Some Christians have received life from Jesus but are still bound by old habits, relationships and attitudes. Peter names four filthy attitudes that we need to take off like a dirty shirt:

- Meanness.
- Pretence.
- Envy.
- Hurtful Talk.

Filthy Attitude One: Meanness

The two words in English are "malice" and "deceit." In the Greek text, they are used in combination to describe a malicious deceiver. They describe a cheat, that is, someone who cheats in a game but they convey the idea that the cheat was malicious and intended to hurt another.

There are some people who just seem to be born mean and I wish I could say that there were none in the church. In view of all the blessings that Christians have freely received from God, how can they justify their meanness? They are mean because they are spiritual babies who have never grown up in their faith. Grow up and throw away that old mean attitude!

Filthy Attitude Two: Pretence

The English word "hypocrisy" is a transliteration of the Greek word. The word was used for an actor who played a part in a play. Acting is okay on stage, because we all know that actors have to pretend to be another to make the play as real as possible for the audience and no one is deceived. But we must not be hypocrites. We must not pretend to be what we are not. Someone said a hypocrite is someone who complains about the sex and violence on their video recorder. Think about it!

Jesus said harsh words to the Pharisees, the religious hypocrites who were righteous only so that others would admire them and think they were good. Jesus said that whilst outwardly they were like whitewashed tombs, inwardly they were full of rotting, stinking, corpses.

Who are the religious hypocrites today? Are they Christians who:

- Talk about praying but seldom pray?
- Say the Bible is God's Word but seldom read it?

We know that some who never go to church often use the presence of hypocrites in the church as their excuse. There is a need today for Christians to get rid of pretence and grow up.

Filthy Attitude Three: Envy

This is the attitude of always comparing yourself to others and mentally competing with them.

Do you recognise thoughts that are similar to these?

- I make more money than they do.
- I think I'm thinner than her.
- I doubt that big ring is real.

Would you agree that nothing makes your car depreciate more than when your neighbour buys a newer one?

Have you ever considered the difference between envy and love?

- Envy is quick to see the faults of others and magnify them.
  Love minimises mistakes.
- Envy looks at people through a microscope.
  Love looks through a telescope.

When you are green with envy, you are ripe for trouble. Get rid of it!

Filthy Attitude Four: Hurtful Talk

Slander means to speak words that hurt others. It is putting someone down, either when you are talking to them or about them. Sadly, many Christians have sharp tongues that wound and injure the feelings and reputations of others. A mature Christian would rather bite their tongue than say anything harmful or hurtful.

Filthy Attitudes: A summary

We have considered four sinful attitudes. They were meanness, pretence, envy and hurtful talk. Did you notice that all of them are relational in nature? You cannot be right with God if you are mistreating others. These are all childish sins of immaturity and if present in your life, they are a sign that you need to grow up. The important question that I must now ask you is this. Do you want to grow up?

Let me give you a loving wake-up call. If you have no desire to get rid of these sinful attitudes, you are not a true follower of Jesus. The key word is desire. If you are content with these four filthy sins in your life, then you need to meet Jesus. Do you display attitudes that are found in a nursery? God is asking you to grow up.

A desire for God's Word stimulates your growth

Peter gives us the recipe for growth:

"Like newborn babies, crave pure spiritual milk, so that by it you may grow up in your salvation" 1Peter 2:2

When God gives a negative directive, He always gives a positive one to balance it. So although God say to us there are attitudes that we need to get rid of, He also says there is something that we must have. We need a hunger, a craving to read and study His Word. The word for "crave" means something much stronger than a casual desire. Some cravings are bad for us and I do not need to tell you about the real dangers of alcohol and drugs. But did you realise that we should crave for the Bible like:

- An alcoholic craves alcohol?
- A drug addict craves for a fix?

We should have a good obsessive addiction to read and study God's Word. The word "crave" that Peter uses in verse 2 is the same word the Psalmist uses in Psalm 42 where we read:

"As the deer pants for the streams of water, so my soul pants for you, O God." Psalm 42:1

Have you seen an animal so thirsty that it is panting? Can you sincerely claim that you have that level of desire in your relationship with God and His Word?

Peter compares spiritual hunger to the way new born babies crave milk. We should crave God's Word the way a baby craves milk. Milk is a powerful analogy for God's Word. God's Word is the only food recommended by God for Christians who want to stop being babies and grow up. But too many Christians seem content with what I call "spiritual junk food." Here are some of the most popular:

The McBible

Ideal for Christians who:

- Only eat spiritual fast food.
- Only want to flip the Bible open and gulp down a verse or two on the run.
- Foolishly say: "A verse a day keeps the devil away."
- Never bother about their spiritual indigestion.

The Church Bell Drive-Through Bible

Suitable for Christians who:

- Make a weekly run for their spiritual take-away on Sundays.
- Do not mind eating unhealthily.
- Have and only want a pre-processed faith and loads of re-fried blessings.
- Will not admit that they starve during the week or, if they do not, admit what other junk food they have been buying and eating and where it came from.

The Boil in the Bag Bible

Perfect for Christians who:

- Sit at home and only ever watch church on television.
- Never meet with other Christians for times of worship and fellowship and to study the Bible.

- Are selfish and must have things done their way.
- Would only consider going back to church if everything was done the way they like it.

The Candyfloss Bible

Designed for those people who:
- Talk about God or "the Good Lord."
- Never read the Bible to find out what God is really like.
- Have no idea what God requires of them.

I hope that my "popular spiritual junk foods" comments made you smile but I had a serious purpose in writing as I did because I need to stress that if you are going to grow toward maturity, you are going to have to quit eating spiritual junk food and start feasting on God's Word. The great British preacher, Charles Haddon Spurgeon wrote:

"A true Christian would rather go without a meal than without a sermon. He would sooner miss a meal than lose his daily portion of Scripture or his daily resort to the house of prayer."

It is normal to be a spiritual infant for a brief period after you are born again but you must then grow up. You will not grow unless you feed on God's Word regularly. Paul was frustrated with the church at Corinth because it was full of spiritual babies who were not growing up. Paul wrote:

"I could not address you as spiritual but as worldly - mere infants in Christ. I gave you milk, not solid food, for you were not ready for it." 1Corinthians 3:1

Paul refers to milk and solid food. I consider that if you have been a Christian for four or more years, you should be feeding on the meat, not the milk, of the Word. Are you able to digest meat? Many have been followers of Jesus for years and they ought to be teaching newly born believers the things of God. But what do we find? They are still being bottle-fed week after week themselves.

Friendship with Jesus as Lord supports your growth

"Grow up in your salvation, now that you have tasted that the Lord is good." 1Peter 2:3

I love these words of Peter because the reason we want to keep on growing in our salvation is that we have had a taste of experiencing God and we know from personal experience that God is good. A thousand years earlier, David wrote about the first divine taste test:

"Oh, taste and see that the Lord is good. Blessed is the man who takes refuge in him." Psalm 34:8

Peter is writing to people like us who have already participated in that taste test.

Can you remember when you tasted something delicious for the first time? Let me tell you about my experience of a pomegranate. I can still recall that first bite. I tossed about a dozen of those luscious red seeds in my mouth and bit down. There was an explosion of flavour that touched taste buds that had been dormant in my mouth for years! A delicious taste! Before that experience, if you had asked me if pomegranates were good, I would have said, "I do not know" because I had never had a personal encounter with a pomegranate. But now I can tell you about my personal experience because I have eaten one.

If you ask me, "Is God good?" I can answer, "Yes." God's goodness is something I have personally experienced! Have you? If you have tasted the goodness of the Lord, you will never be satisfied with anything less! You will have a craving to:

- Continually grow.
- Keep on experiencing the goodness of God.

Our spiritual growth is a never ending journey so that while we are alive we will never have:

Found out all there is to know about God.
Become as mature as we can ever be.

We are like "work in progress." Many of you will be familiar with that technical term used in production management to describe something that needs more work to be done on it before it can be classed as completed, finished or perfect. Jesus is the One who is working on us and in us. Paul wrote:

"... being confident of this, that he who began a good work in you will carry it on to completion until the day of Christ Jesus." Philippians 1:6

In order to keep growing you must:

- Want to grow.
- Believe you can grow.

Some Christians get into a rut and I often say that a rut is only a grave with no ends. They think that spiritual life or growth beyond where they are at the moment is impossible. They are guilty of what John Piper calls, "Spiritual Fatalism." He writes:

"Spiritual fatalism is a great threat to spiritual growth. It is the belief or feeling that you are stuck with the way you are. It is a feeling that genetic forces and family forces and the forces of my past experiences are just too strong to allow me to ever change and become more zealous, more fervent, more joyful, or more hopeful in God." John Piper.

Would you say to a gawky 13 year old who was disappointed with the shape of their body that they will always look like that because that is how they look now? Of course you would not! Children are meant to grow and change.

While it could be harmful to tell a child that it will never grow up, sooner or later the child will discover the truth and as the child grows, it will be able to monitor growth very accurately. Spiritual fatalism is extremely harmful because spiritual growth, unlike physical growth, cannot be measured as we never get to a point where we have arrived at our final stature. Many Christians live year after year in ruts that make spiritual growth impossible. Many stay in their ruts because they do not realise that they could leave them if they had the desire to do so. Many have no desire, no:

- Passion for God.
- Zeal for God's Name.
- Joy in God's presence.

Are you one of them? Do you think, "Well, that is just the way I am?" Do you just settle for what you have? Why be like a child when you could grow up? Why live with pimples until you die? Get out of your spiritual rut now.

How to Grow-A Practical Programme

I hope you are now convinced that you need to grow up spiritually. I want to tell you how you start to grow and keep growing.

A man walked up to a vending machine and put his coin into the slot. He pressed the button that said, "Coffee, Cream and Sugar." No cup appeared but there was a whirring noise and nozzles went into action sending down a flow of coffee, cream and sugar. After it had all gone down the drain the machine turned itself off. The man said, "Now, that is automation! Not only does this machine make your coffee, it drinks it for you!"

It would be nice if spiritual growth was automatic but it is not. Spiritual growth involves more than a desire to grow. It also needs discipline. There are some things that you need to know and to do to start growing and keep growing. The Christian life is like riding a bicycle. If you stop pedalling, you will definitely fall over. There are four things you must do daily and you can remember them by the four letters in the word "G.R.O.W." They are:

- Get the prayer habit.
- Read God's Word.
- Others have needs.
- Work for Jesus.

Get the prayer habit

If you make a commitment to spend time in prayer daily, you will grow. Let me clarify this for some misunderstand what prayer is. I am not talking about repeating memorised prayers. I am talking about praying and that means talking to God.

Read God's Word

Every single day you need to read a portion of the Bible. Growing involves more than showing up for Bible Study and Worship once a week. Growing requires a personal discipline that makes time for daily prayer and Bible Study so that you stay connected to God. I suggest you carry a copy of God's Word with you. Read it whenever you have a spare moment. You must also obey what it says. Become 'a doer' of the Word. Use it as a mirror and your life will be changed by it.

Others have needs

That is a reminder that every single day you relate to the people around you. You will meet only two kinds of people. There are believers and non-believers. It is a good idea to regard non-believers as pre-believers. The believers you meet need you and you need them for fellowship. Those who are not yet believers need you to show them the love of Jesus.

Work for Jesus

A great way to grow is to get involved in some kind of ministry. Most immature Christians are pew potatoes.

They come to church and sit and soak and sour. They are not participators in the work of God. Some would not even qualify as spectators. If you are a pew potato, get up and get involved in some kind of ministry.

I guarantee that if you work consistently on those four areas you will move toward spiritual maturity. You will never reach a point where you stop growing. Now you know what to do. But remember, having a burning passion to grow toward maturity is the key.

Chapter 9

How To Pray

I love the way children pray. We can learn from their simplicity. Here are two examples to make you smile before we consider how to pray:

Dear God, I bet it's very hard for you to love all the people in the world. There are only four in our family and I can never do it.

Dear God, thank you for my baby brother but what I prayed for was a puppy.

One of the bestselling books in recent years is The Prayer of Jabez. In the book, Bruce Wilkinson examines a prayer from First Chronicles 4 prayed by Jabez. This twenty-nine word prayer is used as an example and the reader is encouraged to pray it daily. I appreciate any book that encourages people to pray more but I prefer the Prayer of Jesus.

The following verses are often called The Lords' Prayer or the Model Prayer as I prefer to call it. I prefer it to the Prayer of Jabez because Jesus knew more about prayer than Jabez could ever have known!

I hope it is your desire to say the same thing the disciples said to Jesus, "Lord, teach us to pray."

Both Matthew and Luke refer to the Model Prayer, so I am quoting from both of them, Matthew first:

"This, then, is how you should pray: "'Our Father in heaven, hallowed be your name, your kingdom come, your will be done on earth as it is in heaven. Give us today our daily bread. Forgive us our debts, as we also have forgiven our debtors. And lead us not into temptation, but deliver us from the evil one.'" Matthew 6:9-13

"One day Jesus was praying in a certain place. When he finished, one of his disciples said to him, "Lord, teach us to pray, just as John taught his disciples." He said to them, "When you pray, say: "'Father, hallowed be your name, your kingdom come. Give us each day our daily bread. Forgive us our sins, for we also forgive everyone who sins against us. And lead us not into temptation.'" Luke 11:1-4

Dozens of people have said to me through the years that they do not think their prayers are getting past the ceiling and in frustration, some quit praying. Let me ask you three questions that will help you to prepare for what I have to tell you about prayer.

Question 1

You walk into a room, flip the light switch and nothing happens. Do you say:

"Thomas Edison was a liar? That's it. No more electric lights for me?"
My Answer: Of course not! I know that you would never say anything so foolish and neither would anyone else.

Question 2

So what do you do when the lights do not work?

My Answer: You start thinking about the problem and how you can fix it. You ask yourself questions such as:

1. "What's wrong?"
2. "What needs fixing?"
3. "Does the bulb needs replacing?"
4. "Has a fuse blown?"
5. "Has the electricity been shut down in this area?"

Question 3

Why do some people deal with their prayer problems in a totally different manner to their electricity problems?

My Answer: They do not understand that if our prayers are ineffective, there are things we can do to "fix" our prayer problem.

In this prayer that we are going to consider, Jesus gives us His advice, which must be the best advice, on how we can improve our prayer life.

At churches all across the world every Sunday, thousands will recite the Model Prayer but how many really pray? I am convinced that Jesus never intended this prayer to be repeated from memory, without any thought as to what we are praying for. Instead, Jesus gave us a pattern that our prayers should follow.

Those of you who work with word processors know that templates are used for different types of documents. The templates provide a general outline but you must input the information that is required in the appropriate place. The Model Prayer is like a template with six sections. As we pray, we must input what is required in each of the six sections because each section has its own principle that we must follow. So, to pray as Jesus taught us to, we must:

- Recognise God's Character.
- Respect God's Name.
- Request God's Will.
- Rely on God's Provision.
- Reflect God's Forgiveness.
- Remain on God's Pathway.

I want to consider with you each of these six principles.

Principle of Prayer One: Recognise God's Character

"Our Father ..."

If and how you pray will be determined by what you think about God. If you think God is an uninterested, unapproachable tyrant on the other side of the universe, you will think praying is a waste of time.

Jesus taught that God is like a loving Father and that concept of God is unique to the Christian Faith.

Jesus' most revolutionary statements were His claim to:

- Come from Heaven.
- Have a Heavenly Father.

"Father" was His favourite designation for God. He referred to God as "Father" one hundred and seventeen times in the Gospel of John. The only time that Jesus did not use the term "Father" was when He was on the cross and called out, "My God, my God why have you forsaken me?"

People mention the "fatherhood of God" over all people. It is known as Universalism and it is a lie. Jesus did not teach it and made it abundantly clear that God is not the Father of everyone, only those who have been born again and made a part of His family. By way of contrast we read that Jesus said to the Pharisees:

"You belong to your father, the devil, and you want to carry out your father's desire. He was a murderer from the beginning." John 8:44

So there are two spiritual fathers and two spiritual families on this earth. If you have trusted Jesus as your personal Saviour, you can rejoice that God is your Father and He relates to you the way a loving father relates to his child.

Pater was the formal word for father that Jesus often used when speaking of God but He also called God, "Abba," a tender word of affection that a child would use, like our word "daddy." Paul writes:

For you did not receive a spirit that makes you a slave again to fear, but you received the Spirit of Sonship. And by him we cry, "Abba, Father." Romans 8:15

Jesus taught us that when we pray, we can talk to God as a child would talk to a loving Father. That is why I do not care for "flowery prayers" that use a lot of artificial words. Some people do not pray vocally, even in small groups, because they have heard preachers and others pray and have concluded that special words and phrases are needed to pray "properly" or "the right way." I have never understood why preachers talk normally when they preach but when they pray, they sound as if they have swallowed an old-fashioned Bible Dictionary. It came as no surprise to me that the answer to a crossword clue was "Amen." The question was: An eagerly awaited word.

Imagine this scenario: A family walk past a kiosk and one of the children wants some ice cream. How does the child speak to the dad? Does the child say? "Hail, thou eminent and wise school teacher. Wouldest thou grant to thy offspring an appropriate coin so that I mightest purchase from yon kiosk one ice cream cornet with a chocolate flake therein to tickle the taste buds of my tender mouth?" No, the child says, "Dad, may I have please have some money for an ice cream?" That shows not only respect but trust. Understanding that God is your loving Father will affect the way you approach Him and how you address Him.

Principle of Prayer Two: Respect God's Name

"Hallowed be Your Name ..."

One child said He knew God's name, it was Harold. He had heard them say in church, "Harold be your name"!

Unless we talk about the "hallowed halls" of some very old building, most of us would not use the word "hallowed" at all in our everyday vocabulary but in this prayer, it is an important word that we need to think about. It simply means:

- "Holy" or "special."

God is not only our Loving Father. He is:

- A Holy God.
- Worthy of our praise.

Jesus is teaching a pattern here. It is good to begin prayer with praise. Praise is bragging about God's character. You can do that in your own words or you can sing a song of praise. Also, in your personal prayer time, it would be a good idea to read a Psalm of praise to God. Many of the Psalms contain words of pure praise. Let me give you an example. The first two verses of Psalm 93 read:

"The Lord reigns, he is robed in majesty; the Lord is robed in majesty and is armed with strength. The world is firmly established it cannot be moved. Your throne was established long ago; you are from all eternity." Psalm 93:1-2:

You should:

- Praise God for Who He is.
- Thank God for what He is done.

Every human father loves to be both praised and thanked by his children and when our children ask us for things and thank us, it blesses us. But if they brag about us, it blesses us in an even greater way. You can bless God by bragging about Him!

A father I know had a card from his daughter with these words. "I am constantly amazed at how fortunate I am to be your daughter." She ended by writing, "You will always be the first man I loved! Do you think he was blessed? In the same way, your Heavenly Father is blessed when you praise Him. Before you ask for anything, spend some prayer time bragging about the greatness of God.

Principle of Prayer Three: Request God's Will

"Your Kingdom come ..."

Note that this is the first request in the Model Prayer. We ask God to establish His Kingdom on earth. The phrase "Your will be done on earth as it is in Heaven" that we read in Matthew 6:10 is not an additional request to "Your Kingdom come" but a clarification of it. Let me explain it to you like this:

- God's Kingdom is established whenever and wherever His will is done.

- God is King of Heaven and therefore His perfect will is always done there.
- God's Kingdom is established in your life and mine when we commit ourselves to God and live obedient to His will and not our own.
- When Jesus told us to "seek first the Kingdom of God," He meant that we are to choose to follow God's Will for our lives.

The concept of "the will of God" is so misunderstood in our world. For instance, some people have such a fatalistic, fixed idea of the will of God that they say everything that happens is the will of God. So what is the will of God and how is it relevant to our lives? These are the truths that you will find in the Bible:

- God is sovereign because He created everything and therefore there is no higher authority than God.
- God is in control of everything that He created.
- God loves us so much that:
  - He has given everyone a very dangerous capacity that we know as "choice".
  - He did not create us as robots that automatically always do His will.
- Evil came into the world when man sinned and it has had a devastating effect upon and spoilt God's perfect creation. Terrible global consequences have resulted to a creation that God made for our good.

People so easily blame God for these disasters, some even calling them "Acts of God," but that is because they do not realise the extent to which evil impacted our planet.

- Sinful people make evil choices. There are always terrible consequences to face when evil choices are made.

In this Model Prayer, Jesus teaches a powerful principle. God's will is always done in Heaven but not on earth. So we must pray for God's will to be done on earth and then we must do it! If you are a fatalist, I want to ask you this. If everything that happens or has happened on earth is or has been God's will, why would Jesus instruct us to pray for God's will to be done on earth?

God will not force His will on anyone. No one gets out of bed and goes to church like zombies who have no control over their decisions. No, we choose to get up and to follow God's will by assembling with others to worship as His Word directs.

We are living in a world where God's will is not done much of the time and that is why we are called upon to pray for His Kingdom to come. Only when God's Kingdom comes into our lives and into this world will God's will be done on earth as it is in Heaven.

There is another matter that I want to mention while we are thinking about God's will. God's will is connected or linked to His Word. Think of it like this.

If someone wants to know what your will or desire is, you can tell them or write it out. But you do not want them presuming to know what your will is. God clearly states His will in His Word, the Bible and that is why we must study it to determine what His will is.

It is as silly as it is dangerous for us to presume to know the will of God. We study God's Word and then pray that His will be done. But we must be willing to do God's will ourselves.

Principle of Prayer Four: Rely on God's Provision

"Give us each day …"
This part of the Model Prayer teaches two vital truths:

- It is God who supplies all our needs.
- You must depend upon God's provision every day.

It is God who supplies all our needs, even the most basic need of food. Every day we are to trust Him and to ask Him to provide whatever we need. Paul writes:

"And my God will meet all your needs according to his glorious riches in Christ Jesus." Philippians 4:19

Paul wrote "all your needs" not "all your wants." Every time you pause to pray before a meal you acknowledge God supplied the food and the money to buy the food.

A wonderful Bible Teacher of a previous century was Dr. H. A. Ironside. He once ate in a restaurant that was so crowded that he had to sit at a table with a stranger. Before he ate, Dr. Ironside asked the stranger if he might pray. The stranger said, "Go ahead. But I do not ever pray before I eat. I just jump right in and eat." With a smile, Dr. Ironside said, "You know, that is exactly what my dog does." Then He proceeded to pray and he was able to talk to the man about Christ as they ate.

There is also significance in the phrase "each day." Jesus was teaching we must depend upon God's provision every single day. We stockpile our freezers with food to last us for many days but prayer does not work that way. You cannot stockpile your prayers. You know the story in the Old Testament about God feeding the wandering Israelites with manna from heaven. Each day, except the Sabbath, they had to go out and collect a fresh supply because yesterday's manna was always full of maggots and it stank. Yesterday's prayers are no good for you today. The key to effective praying is setting aside a time every day to spend time with God. We often call that 'a quiet time'.

Certainly you ought to pray before you eat and whenever you lie down in bed but it is best to set aside a special time to focus on God in prayer. That was the habit of Jesus. Mark 1 verse 35 tells us that Jesus got up before daylight and went out to a solitary place to pray. Our world is so busy and there are so many demands that create stress, that a quiet time is not just a good idea, it is a necessity. C.S. Lewis wrote:

"The moment you wake up each morning, all your wishes and hopes for the day rush at you like wild animals. And the first job each morning consists in shoving it all back; in listening to that other voice, taking that other point of view, letting that other, larger, stronger, quieter life come flowing in."

Principle of Prayer Five: Reflect God's Forgiveness

"Forgive us our sins..."

One reason I do not like the term "The Lord's Prayer" is because I do not believe that Jesus prayed this prayer. The Bible teaches us that He was totally sinless so He had no need to ask for forgiveness. Instead it is a "Model Prayer" because each of us desperately needs God's forgiveness. We have all sinned and we continue to make mistakes and experience failure. Jesus recognised that the greatest need a person has is to be forgiven.

In Luke 5 there is an incident recorded in which four friends tore up the roof to lower their paralysed friend in front of Jesus. All of us would have looked at the man and claimed his greatest need was for physical healing but Jesus looked at him and said, "Friend, your sins are forgiven." Look at any crowd of people. You will see people who you think have certain needs and you will see people who you think do not need anything. But

Jesus looks at each of us and says, "You need forgiveness." When you are born again, the penalty of sin, separation from God for eternity, is removed once and forever. But the presence of sin in our lives is still a reality. Even though we have a new nature, our flesh is constantly dragging us back into sin. A Christian may sin but a true Christian cannot sin and enjoy it.

There is a key point in this prayer that people miss. This is what Jesus was actually teaching us to pray and note the italics: "Forgive us our sins *in the same way that* we forgive those who sin against us." Jesus made it perfectly clear in Matthew 6:

"If you forgive men when they sin against you, your heavenly Father will also forgive you. But if you do not forgive men their sins, your Father will not forgive your sins." Matthew 6:14-15

Those verses do not teach that you can earn God's forgiveness by forgiving others. However, when you have truly experienced God's forgiveness for your own sin against God, you will reflect that forgiveness to anyone who has sinned against you. You will appreciate that, as your sin against a holy God is so horrendous, no one will ever sin against you as badly as you have sinned against God and He has forgiven you. Once you have realised that the cost of your forgiveness was the death of God's precious Son Jesus on the cross, how can you not forgive others? Your willingness to forgive others is a proof of your salvation not a prerequisite.

Did you know that any unconfessed sin short-circuits your prayer life? That is why you flip the "prayer switch" and nothing happens. What must you do first?

- See if there is sin in your life that you are hanging onto.

David wrote:

"If I had cherished sin in my heart, the Lord would not have listened." Psalm 66:18

I have found that whenever I have asked God to tell me if there is some sin or attitude in my life that is not pleasing to Him, He has always told me.

Principle of Prayer Six: Remain on God's Pathway

"Lead us not into temptation ..."

These words have often been misunderstood. They literally mean this: "Lead us, lest we fall into temptation and deliver us from the Evil One." God cannot lead you into temptation. James wrote:

"When tempted, no one should say, "God is tempting me." For God cannot be tempted by evil, nor does he tempt anyone; but each one is tempted when, by his own evil desire, he is dragged away and enticed." James 1:14

God's pathway never leads to sin. It is our own evil desires that make us want to leave God's pathway of purity and go off onto some roadway of ruin. Prayer helps you remain on God's pathway.

The devil or Satan is the evil one and he hates it when a Christian prays. Samuel Chadwick wrote:

"The one concern of the devil is to keep Christians from praying. He fears nothing from prayerless studies, prayerless work, and prayerless religion. He laughs at our toil, mocks at our wisdom but he trembles when we pray." Samuel Chadwick.

And Charles Hendon Spurgeon wrote:

"I would rather teach one man to pray than to teach ten men to preach." C. H. Spurgeon.

As you journey through life, you will be tempted off God's pathway to take some enticing detour. Every day you and I are confronted with decisions about different pathways to follow. The vast majority of people in this world are on pathways of their own choosing or design, or else on that popular pathway of "being like everyone else." Robert Frost wrote a poem entitled, The Road Not Taken, in which the final lines read:

"Two roads diverged in a wood, and I –
I took the one less travelled by,
And that's made all the difference."
Robert Frost

God's pathway seems to be less travelled along, these days. When you pray, will you tell God that you desire His leadership and will follow His pathway?

Some criticise the Model Prayer thinking that they have found a flaw in it. They say that it is a selfish prayer because it does not contain prayers for others. They are wrong because Jesus used plural pronouns when He said, "Give us... Lead us... Forgive us ...." Jesus did not teach us to say, "Give me... Lead me... Forgive me..."

Some have left God's pathway. Have you? Is this one of your poor choices? God is calling you to follow Him again. Will you get back on track now? Confess your sins and start following His will as you discover it in His Word. Where does God's pathway lead? Let the Bible and David, the Shepherd King who knew so much about sheep that wandered away from the shepherd, answer:

"The LORD is my shepherd. He gives me everything I need. He makes me lie down in green pastures, he leads me beside quiet waters, he restores my soul. He guides me in the paths of righteousness for his name's sake." Psalm 23:1-3

- Has wandering away from God's pathway left you spiritually hungry and weary? Do you need to eat fresh and tender grass and then lie down and rest in the green pastures that God has provided for you?
- Are you drinking from and drowning in troubled waters when God has provided spiritual waters that

are restful and peaceful for those who are on His pathway?

- Has going-it alone been unsuccessful and left you both mentally and physically worn-out? Do you now need leading to where there are still, quiet waters?

Is it righteousness that you need? We have none of our own and the Bible deflates the opinions of any who claim to be good by likening self-righteousness to filthy rags. If you get on God's pathway you will find Jesus. Jesus will take your sins and He will give you His righteousness in exchange. The Bible says:

"God made him who had no sin to be sin for us, so that in him we might become the righteousness of God."
2Corinthians 5:21

The Model Prayer is far more than just a prayer. It is a guide that will help to put you and keep you on God's pathway to eternal life.

Chapter 10

How To Tackle Bad News

Cliff was in a hot air balloon and lost. He reduced altitude and spotting a woman shouted to her, "Where am I? I promised to meet a friend an hour ago." She replied, "You are in a balloon 31 feet above the ground, between forty and forty-one degrees north latitude and between fifty-nine and sixty degrees west longitude." "You are an engineer," he said. "How did you know?" she replied. He answered, "What you said is technically correct but frankly not much help." She responded, "You are in management." "How did you know?" he replied. "It is obvious," she said. "You do not know where you are or where you are going. You have risen to where you are due only to a large quantity of hot air. You make promises and have no idea how to keep them. You expect people beneath you to solve your problems and you are in exactly the same position you were in before we met but now, you blame me."

No one needs to tell me that life has become complex for everyone. Almost daily it seems that we are forced to figure out how to handle:

- Bad news.
- Impossible problems.
- Clever enemies.

I do not know your circumstances but I would be surprised if your life was problem-free. Those who are now will not stay for long in that state. Christians are no different from unbelievers because no one can belong to God without passing through trials and discipline.

You know your own circumstances. My intention in this chapter is not to encourage self-pity. Self-pity is dangerous. It makes problems worse and causes further distress. I want to encourage you to have a realistic assessment of your problems so that you can learn from God's Word how to handle them. The story of how King Hezekiah dealt with his problems will help you.

When Hezekiah was in trouble, there were four options available to him. He could have:

- Faced the problem on his own.
- Become resentful and angry toward God.
- Turned to other gods.
- Simply given up.

So let us consider Hezekiah's problems and what he did. The account of how Hezekiah dealt with his problems is found in Second Kings 18 and 19. He was a King of Judah and he lived some seven hundred years before Jesus. His father was Ahaz, one of the wickedest of the Judean Kings. In that strange pattern that sometimes emerges, we see Hezekiah, born of godless parents, become one of the godliest Kings to reign in Judah:

- He ascended the Throne at Jerusalem when he was twenty-five and he reigned for twenty-nine years.
- He smashed the idols and worshiped the Lord.
- He observed the Commandments given by Moses and lived in a manner that was totally different from the ways of his father.

But life was not particularly good to Hezekiah:

- The Assyrians were at the peak of their power.
- They had conquered the northern Kingdom of Israel.
- Israel's capital Samaria had fallen to the powerful Shalmaneser at the end of a three-year siege, at a time when Hezekiah had been King of Judah for only four years.
- Eleven years later, Sennacherib turned against Judah and captured its fortified cities.
- Hezekiah begged for Sennacherib's understanding but to no avail.
- Hezekiah stripped the Treasury of the Temple and the King's House to pay tribute but Sennacherib was

not satisfied. His lust for greater power and money had taken control.

This Bible history is confirmed by the fact that archaeologists have discovered the "Taylor Cylinder" in which King Sennacherib bragged about capturing forty-six cities of Judah, taking over two hundred thousand captives in addition to a huge number of cattle and beasts of every kind. Hezekiah paid literally millions of pounds worth of gold and silver to Sennacherib but he wanted more. Hezekiah had initially been willing to pay the tribute and had accommodated the Assyrian invaders up to a point but we read that Sennacherib now demanded the surrender of Jerusalem.

- Sennacherib sent Rabshakeh and his other military aides to the gates of Jerusalem.
- The Assyrians sneered at the Jews and laughed at the possibility of a Jewish-Egyptian alliance.
- They mocked God and even claimed to be prompted by God who, they said, had told them to attack Judah and destroy it.

During negotiations, Hezekiah's aides begged the Assyrians not to speak in Hebrew because they feared that the threats they were uttering might upset the Jewish soldiers and the people who could hear the negotiations. Rabshakeh's response was:

"'Was it only to your master and you that my master sent me to say these things, and not to the men sitting on the wall—

who, like you, will have to eat their own filth and drink their own urine?'" Then Rabshakeh called out in a loud voice in the Hebrew language, urging the people to listen to the great king of Assyria. "Hear the word of the great king, the king of Assyria! This is what the king says: Do not let Hezekiah deceive you. He cannot deliver you from my hand. Do not let Hezekiah persuade you to trust in the Lord when he says, 'The Lord will surely deliver us: this city will not be given into the hand of the king of Assyria.'" 2Kings 18:27-30

Rabshakeh told the people that if they surrendered they would prosper. They might be taken into captivity but they would still have a good life. By directing their propaganda at the people, the enemy tried to create internal problems for Hezekiah. Eliakim and Joah tore their clothes and brought the terrible words of Rabshakeh to Hezekiah. Hezekiah's world tumbled in!

Have you ever come to a point when your world has fallen apart? When this happens, how do you handle the downs of life, your bad news, your impossible problems and your clever enemies?

I want to consider with you the four options that were available to Hezekiah at the time of his problems. You will recall that he could have:

- Faced the problem on his own.
- Become resentful and angry toward God.
- Turned to other gods.
- Simply given up.

Do you try to face problems on your own?

Are you one of those think, "When the going gets tough, the tough get going?" You may win some of the time because you are clever enough to draw on your own innate human resources and you might do a pretty good job. But for how long can you fight? Some fight for a while and then, when they run out of their own resources, find that things get worse.

Let me give you an example of a recurring and increasingly frequent problem to illustrate my point. It might be that you feel that your wife is cold. Some other woman is warm. Your wife will not change, so you change the ground rules from "'til death do us part" to "'til I do not get what I want." The alienation gets deeper. Now the children are looking at you with those puzzled eyes.

You know that you did not really mean to get in the jam you are in. You thought you could handle it in your own strength. After all, you have handled just about every other problem in life with a good degree of success. But how does your tough stance cope now?

Do you become resentful and angry toward God?

Maybe your husband has gone or you face the loneliness of death and your children do not care. Your new neighbourhood is not as friendly as the town you came from.

Do you say to yourself:

- How could a good God allow me to be so unsuccessful with my life?
- Is the Christian Faith what it claims to be?

You are on a self-pity trip and like many today, you find it so easy to blame God for the problems of life.
Do you turn to other gods?

Both Hezekiah's father, Ahaz and Hezekiah's son Manasseh turned to other gods:

- Ahaz and Manasseh did what was evil in the sight of the Lord. They turned to the Canaanite gods and built "high places, erecting alters for Baal."
- Manasseh even burned his own son as an offering, practiced soothsaying and augury and dealt with mediums and wizards.

Cultic religion has a weird fascination for people who are troubled or have problems. Do you seek comfort in reading horoscope predictions or the "Your Stars" features that now seem to be in every paper and magazine? Astrology, fortune-telling and the like are all forbidden by God.

Do you just give up?

Intelligent and powerful people such as Rabshakeh will urge you to raise the white flag. They will say, "You have done your best, pal. Just give up."

We have now considered four ways of dealing with problems. Let me review them with you.

Hezekiah could have:

- Faced the problem on his own.
- Become resentful and angry toward God.
- Turned to other gods.
- Simply given up.

I am quite certain that Hezekiah was tempted toward these options because so many are. But Hezekiah:

- Stopped.
- Assessed the situation.
- Took a better option.

By his approach to problems, Hezekiah shows you and me how to handle bad news, impossible problems and clever enemies. We see it reflected in the way our story unravels:

- Hezekiah is at his lowest point.
- He sees no way out.
- Not only have the Assyrians mocked him publicly but knowing that he was a man of God, they send him a

letter specifically warning him what will happen to him if he trusts God.

- The Assyrians specifically mention the names of the nations which Assyria had already destroyed.
- Rabshakeh also raises the rhetorical question:

"'Did the gods of the nations that were destroyed by my forefathers deliver them: the gods of Gozan, Haran, Rezeph and the people of Eden who were in Tel Assar? Where is the King of Hamath, the King of Arpad, the King of the city of Sepharvaim, or of Hena or Ivvah?'" 2Kings 19:12-13

Hezekiah did not accept any of the options we have considered. Instead, this is what he did:

"Hezekiah received the letter from the messengers and read it. Then he went up to the temple of the LORD and spread it out before the LORD. And Hezekiah prayed to the LORD: "O LORD, God of Israel, enthroned between the cherubim, you alone are God over all the kingdoms of the earth. You have made heaven and earth. Give ear, O LORD, and hear; open your eyes, O LORD, and see; listen to the words Sennacherib has sent to insult the living God." 2Kings 19:14-16

I do not know any other passage of Scripture that I find more exhilarating in its example of how we are to handle the impossible situations of life. I urge you to take a good, hard look at Hezekiah's situation:

- He is at the lowest point of his life.
- He has paid the price of being a reformer for God.
- He has humbled himself before a mighty military power by paying tribute.

- A number of his cities have been captured.
- He has been belittled publicly.
- He has received a personal, threatening message.

What would we have done in Hezekiah's situation? Would that letter, that personal, threatening message from your powerful enemy, have been the last straw for you and me? What did Hezekiah do? He read it and he went up to the House of the Lord with it. He spread the letter and the whole problem before the Lord.

What Hezekiah did should not be underestimated because this is what prayer is all about. It is about taking and spreading out before the Lord the most:

- Intimate details of your life.
- Personal and precious things in your life.
- Threatening problems that you have ever faced.

I do hope that you share my enthusiasm as I read this story of Hezekiah. I cannot get it out of my mind because the essential thrust of this passage is that you and I are privileged to be able to take our problems and lay them out before the Lord. I want you to note that as Hezekiah does this he takes six vital steps that we would be wise to copy. We read that Hezekiah:

- Humbled himself.
- Entered the House of God.
- Shared his problems with fellow believers.

- Directed his prayer to God.
- Reviewed his problem with the Lord.
- Entrusted his whole life into God' hands.

First: He humbled himself

"...Hezekiah....tore his clothes and put on sackcloth and went into the temple of the LORD." 2Kings 19:1

You could argue that Hezekiah's circumstances forced him to humble himself but do people in trouble become humble? It must be rare because experience teaches that most cover their difficulties with a cocky, arrogant spirit. We fake it as we try to convince ourselves and others that everything is okay when actually the time has long gone when we should have admitted our need.

The Jews have a wonderful tradition. The celebration of their New Year, Yom Kippur, is a time of celebration. But, it begins with a time of humbling. The faithful Jew examines his life to see if he has wronged anyone and if so, seeks forgiveness. Only when he has humbled himself does the celebration begin.

Second: He entered the House of God

The House of God is representative of an institution we know today as the Church. I think it is appropriate to give a word of caution before we consider this matter of the church. We live in an individualistic age when it is now not uncommon for us to criticise and have little regard for both authority and those institutions that have become part of the fabric of the society we live in.

Our parents respected authority but education and the legal freedoms enjoyed by the media have encouraged us to think for ourselves so we challenge authority and evaluate for ourselves those matters that impact on our lives. One harmful consequence of this change has been that so much of contemporary faith in God today is both lacking in respect and anti-institutional. Hence my word of caution because you are heading for spiritual problems:

- When you think that you can live in fellowship with God but worship alone.
- Talk to God independently of the people of God, the church.

This may initially come as a shock to those of you who know me because for many times I have urged you to take any problem at any time in any place to the Lord. So do not misunderstand the specific point that I am making about fellowship in prayer.

The Bible teaches that:

- We have direct access to God at any time, wherever we are and God does talk directly to us.

- There were two institutions established for the benefit of God's people. They were:
  - The Temple for Old Testament times.
  - The Church for today.
- God is a Spirit:
  - He is everywhere.
  - You do not have to travel to Jerusalem to worship or prayer to Him on Mount Zion, or anywhere else, as Jesus so clearly pointed out to the woman at the well in John 4.
- Jesus established His Church two thousand years ago. It is composed of all those who through the years have repented and put their faith and trust in Him. If you are a believer, you automatically became a member of the church at the moment of your conversion.

The church today:

- We know that there are real problems for unbelievers who come into contact with Christianity because today so many have little biblical knowledge, if any.
- Believers know that the word "church" in the New Testament usually refers to the people of God who meet together in a particular place.
- Many unbelievers think that both the congregation and their place of worship is a church.

- Some unbelievers just simply regard anything to do with Christianity as "the church," whether it is local, national or international.

I do accept and deeply regret that some have made what both believers and unbelievers would regard as "the local church" appear to be both cold and sterile, if not in some localities, dying.

But whatever the views of unbelievers, you know that it is not the people, the building, an institution or a tradition that believers worship. So, whatever your personal views of the local church are or whatever happened that you consider gives you the right to form an opinion, the believers who meet together in your local church are and will always be God's people. So what relevance does this have for you?

While it is not only when you are with the people of God in the local church that you can worship and talk to God, you have the divinely given privilege of associating with them and no Scriptural authority for separating yourself from them.

If, for whatever reason, you think that you can or should isolate yourself from God's people and "go it alone," let me remind you that it was:

- Jesus who established His church.
- Jesus who bought His church with His own blood.

- Through the church that you received the Scriptures, for it was the church that recognised the writings of the prophets and apostles as revealed by the Holy Spirit.
- Through the church that the gospel was passed from generation to generation.

To think that you can grow spiritually outside the context of commitment to others who profess the same faith in Jesus Christ is to deny one of the most important facts of Christian living.

Third: He shared his problems with fellow believers

"He sent Eliakim the palace administrator, Shebna the secretary and the leading priests, all wearing sackcloth, to the prophet Isaiah son of Amoz." 1Kings 19:2

As we know, the Church is composed of the people of God. The Bible makes it clear that they need each other so that they can share problems and grow together bearing one another's burdens. I beg you, whether you have bad news, impossible burdens or you are dealing with some clever enemies, take some faithful Christian friends into your confidence. Please do not try to go it alone. Going it alone will only lead to disaster.

I have to emphasise the importance of forming small groups with three objectives:

- The reading and discussion of the Bible.
- The sharing of personal lives.
- Praying together about matters of personal concern.

I suggest that this is best done in the context of eight to twelve people who meet regularly, claiming the Lord's presence. Granted, it is possible to pray alone. However, your prayer life will take on a new wonderful energy if it connects with other people. It will never have quite the same impact if it is exclusively solitary in nature.

In the book Prayer Can Change Your Life by Dr. William R. Parker is a story of an unusual experiment which applies the methods of modern psychology to the study of prayer. Dr. Parker and his co-author, Elaine St. Johns, were seeking to find out if prayer, rightly understood and practiced, would equal the best psychotherapy for nine months. Forty-five volunteers were carefully divided into three groups of fifteen.

- Group 1 was given the best psychotherapy for remedying emotional disorders in weekly individual counselling sessions.
- Group 2 was made up of people who preferred neither psychotherapy nor prayer therapy. They were to pray alone every night,
- Group 3 was the prayer therapy group. They met weekly for a two-hour session to talk and pray together.

Those in Group 3, the prayer therapy group:

- Received a sealed envelope weekly containing a slip on which was written some undesirable emotion that had been discovered during their therapy sessions and about which they had to pray earnestly for that week only.
- The next week they were given another envelope with another slip.
- There was no suggestion made that the contents of the slips should be shared with the group members.
- Soon the group members began to voluntarily discuss and share their experiences and the progress they were making.

Dr. Parker reported that inhibitions and barriers crumbled as the group recognised that each one needed the help, healing, and encouragement that came from sharing with the group.

All forty-five volunteers were given recognised personality tests to determine what lay in their subconscious that might be a clue to the problems and disturbances found in each one. At the end of nine months, the tests revealed the following improvements:

- Group 1: 65% more treatment desired by the group.
- Group 2: No improvement.
- Group 3: 72% improvement both in symptoms and testing.

The conclusive evidence of spiritual healing was indicated by the fact that all of them wanted to help others as they had been helped.

Fourth: He directed his prayer to God

Hezekiah states the details of his life and his faith as he expresses adoration to God. What he is really doing is expressing what life is all about when he prays:

"...God of Israel, enthroned between the cherubim, you alone are God over all the kingdoms of the earth." 2Kings 19:15

Do you realise what Hezekiah is really saying to God? It will revolutionise your prayer life if you do. He is acknowledging how very special, how unique, the One he is praying to actually is. He is effectively saying:

"I am privileged to be able to speak to the God who created everything there is and who sustains everything there is."

Hezekiah knew that there were many gods that men had made but his God was the only true God and He was not only the God of the whole earth, He was specifically the God of Israel.

But we also note that Hezekiah acknowledges the fact that he is not on his own in dealing with this problem. He has God on his side and God is the ultimate Sovereign of the universe. When you pray, you can also enlarge your prayers by acknowledging who God is. I will guarantee that if your heart is humble before God, you will realise that you are in alliance with the God who will ultimately bring human history to completion in the return of Jesus Christ, the One in whom all human history finds its meaning.

Fifth: He reviewed his problem with the Lord

"Give ear, O LORD, and hear; open your eyes, O LORD, and see; listen to the words Sennacherib has sent to insult the living God." 2Kings 19:16

He is saying: "God, read this letter. What do you think about it?" Hezekiah then reviews for God what Sennacherib has done. Sennacherib has:

- Laid waste nations.
- Cast their gods into the fire, proving that they were just wood and stone made by men's hands and therefore destructible.

Hezekiah may have had a selfish interest to serve but there was more than that in his prayer. Is there more than that in your prayers or do you talk specifically about your bad news? Hezekiah prays:

"'Now, O Lord our God, deliver us from his hand, so that all kingdoms on earth may know that you alone, O Lord, are God.'"2Kings 19:19

Hezekiah is not concerned:

- About his own throne. He knows that some day He will die anyway. If he survives the Assyrians, he could always be overthrown in a palace coup. It had happened before in Judah.

Hezekiah is concerned:

- That the Name of God be not blasphemed. Here is a letter from Sennacherib, mocking God. Hezekiah genuinely wants the Name of God revered. Actually, he is the first king since Solomon that the Scriptures record prayed for this.

Sixth: He entrusted his whole life into God's hands

Let us consider verse 19 again.

"Now, O LORD our God, deliver us from his hand, so that all kingdoms on earth may know that you alone, O LORD, are God." 2Kings 19:19

Hezekiah is saying:

- "I cannot handle my problems alone."
- "I need your help, God. Here I am."
- "What are You going to do to help me?"

It is about this time that the Prophet Isaiah gets back in touch with Hezekiah. He conveys to Hezekiah what God has to say. The Lord has a message for Assyria. God is aware of how Sennacherib has:

- Mocked Him.
- Claimed to have won battles all through the Middle East.

But what Sennacherib did not realise was that God had taken the credit for Sennacherib's victories. When Isaiah spoke to Hezekiah, Isaiah quoted what God had told him. God said that there was not one victory which Sennacherib had won that was not in advance permitted by God. What a classic statement that is of the Sovereignty of God. Now the game is over for Sennacherib. You can read all that God said to him in 2Kings Chapter 19 verses 1-34. Here are two verses:

"'But I know where you stay and when you come and go and how you rage against me. Because you rage against me and your insolence has reached my ears, I will put my hook in your nose and my bit in your mouth, and I will make you return by the way you came.'"1Kings 19:27-28

Then God promised deliverance for Jerusalem and we read that during the night the angel of the Lord slew one hundred and eighty five thousand in the camp of the Assyrians and Sennacherib scurried back home to Nineveh. Soon afterwards, he was worshiping in the house of his own gods, when two of his sons killed him in a palace revolt.

Not all of our troubles are dealt with in quite this time table. It is important for us to realise that our God functions outside of time. God is sovereign, He is in charge.

In spite of all the pains and the hurts, the discouragements and the failures of our lives, "His is the victory!" God's payday is not always Friday.

God already knows your beginning from your end and everything in between. No difficulty has happened to you of which He is unaware. So:

- Spread it all out before Him in humility.
- Involve yourself in His Church.
- Share your problems with fellow believers.
- Acknowledge who He is.
- Review your problems with Him.

Finally, trust the outcome to Him and that requires a vital faith in Jesus Christ.

Chapter 11

How To Manage Money

I am always reading books. I read for my own spiritual growth and I read for just plain fun and when I am travelling. One "fun read" was John Grisham's novel, King of Torts. The main character is a young lawyer working for the poor. One day he is offered a chance to make a great deal of money very quickly on a mass litigation case. He accepts the offer, makes millions almost overnight and then, working on a hot tip, goes after another lucrative case. It is a huge malpractice case that yields him even more millions. The papers dub him, "The King of Torts."

You would think that with all those millions, our hero would be happy but not so. As the months go by, he finds that his fortune causes him a lot of anxiety and stress. As his income increases, so do his expenses and his millions begin to slip through his fingers like sand through an hourglass. Instead of enjoying his money, he worries about it and works even harder to win the next case so that he can acquire even more wealth. By the end of the book the "King of Torts" realises that money can be a source of distress and tension. He learns an important truth. The moral of Grisham's story is that money is not all it is cracked up to be and he is correct because money can bring more pain than pleasure! No matter how much money we have, it can become one of the greatest sources of stress in our lives.

It seems to me that most of us have worried about money from time to time. In fact, one minister took a quick poll of his large congregation. Money is such a sensitive subject that he wisely asked them to close their eyes so that they could vote anonymously when they raised their hands. He asked two questions. The first asked if they had ever been stressed about money. The second asked if their current finances caused frustration. The result was a high majority both times!

A recent poll reports that 64% of all couples worry about money. It is now the main cause of divorce with 51% of all spouses that divorce saying that their finances had something to do with their decision. Some might cynically suggest that we change the marital vows so that the bride and groom pledge to stay together until "debt do us part."

Debt is a big problem that is getting worse. The underlying reasons behind debt are well known and have been the subject of newspaper headlines and stories for some time. Many of us are tempted by adverts and special offers that encourage us to mishandle our money and spend more than we earn. The slip-shod way that many of us handle our money does not just affect our bank accounts. It also affects our walk with the Lord and our obligations to Him and His people. I want to ask three questions and then consider what God's Word says about money management. How can we:

- Avoid money problems?
- Deal with money so that we have less stress?
- Manage money instead of it managing us?

First, we have to understand, and more importantly, firmly believe that:

- All we have belongs to God.
- There is no difference between the sacred and the secular in our lives.
- Our money and the way we handle it are spiritual issues.

We must and can look to God for the answers in this area of our lives. That is what I want to do. I want to go to the Bible for wisdom about money management.

God included a book in the Bible that was written by the wisest and the richest man in the world. He had a great deal of experience managing money. He was King Solomon and he was indeed wealthy. He was so wealthy that he would put the wealthy of today in the shade. For example, the Bible tells us that Solomon ate on plates of solid gold. I mean, when he finished dinner they did not just wash the plates, they polished them. Solomon was incredibly wealthy and God inspired him to share all the wisdom he gleaned from his money management in the book of Proverbs. There are five basic things that Solomon said we must do to manage our money wisely and I want us to look at them. Solomon advises us to:

- Keep good records.
- Plan our spending.
- Save for the future.
- Be content.
- Give to God.

One: Solomon advises us to keep good records

The Principle of Accounting:

Be sure you know the condition of your flocks, give careful attention to your herds; for riches do not endure forever, and a crown is not secure for all generations. Proverbs 27:23-24

In Solomon's day, instead of stocks they had flocks! A man's herds were his assets and it was the shepherd's job to keep track of the size and the condition of the flock. So, in these verses Solomon is saying that to prevent monetary loss and stress, we must keep track of what we have.

You must constantly be aware of the state of your accounts. Are you? Do you say, "I do not know where all my money goes!" Well, if you do not know, then, unless someone is stealing it from you, you are failing to keep good records. As someone has said, "Money used to talk but now it just quietly slips away." You need to keep good records so this does not happen.

Your record keeping must be set up so that it enables you to know four essential things:

Your assets: what you own.
Your income: what you earn.
Your debts: what you owe.
Your expenditure: what you spend your money on.

Software is available for those who can use a computer but if you are like me, just keep a paper record of what comes in and what goes out. Whether you buy groceries or presents, this simple method will enable you to know how much you can afford to spend. It is essential to keep an accurate record of the money that God entrusts to us.

I have found that Solomon is right. Knowing my income and where it goes helps me not to worry about money.

Two: Solomon advises us to plan our spending

The Principle of Budgeting

The plans of the diligent lead to profit as surely as haste leads to poverty. Proverbs 21:5

Your financial freedom will not be determined by how much you earn but by how you spend what you earn. The problem for most of us is that we spend too much. Whether it is at the shops, by catalogue or on the Internet, we spend too much because we shop too much. Did you know that the average person in the west spends six hours a week in shopping-related activities and I guess that many are well above average?

It is wise to shop carefully so that we find the best value for our money. The problem is that many of us do not shop wisely or carefully. Surveys show that nine out of ten of us shop impulsively. We rarely plan our spending and when we do, we do not stick to the plan. We buy more than we intend to but more serious is the fact that we buy more than we can afford to. Why do we do this?

We overspend for various foolish reasons:

- We try to copy wealthier people's lifestyles.
- We try to keep up with our richer neighbours.
- Self-esteem and peer pressure ensure that we must have what our equals have.
- We must have all the latest gadgets.

We are subject to the incredible influence of the media:

- Every advert we see encourages us to buy without any regard to our ability to pay.
- Hour after hour television urges us to Buy! Buy! Buy!

Advertisers are wise. They spend their advertising budgets prudently to get us to waste our money buying their products.

There are constant sales, pressuring us to buy impulsively. I do not know about you but I remember when sales were annual. Now they are every week! Shops and stores now open earlier and stay open later. They promise unbelievable deals which shoppers just cannot resist. Many shoppers admit that they buy goods just because the goods are in the sales.

Let me sum up what I have mentioned about budgeting by asking you a question.

My Question: Is it wise or foolish to buy what you do not need with money you cannot afford?

How would Solomon have answered my question? I can tell you! It is foolish. Solomon said:

"Stupid people spend their money as fast as they get it." Proverbs 21:20

A magazine once did an article called "Are you a shopaholic?" It quoted creative ideas that help people break the habit of impulsive buying. For example, one man kept his credit cards frozen in a chunk of ice in the freezer. If he got the urge to spend, he had to wait for the ice to melt. By then, the urge to buy had gone.

Solomon would say that the best way to break the habit of impulsive buying is by budgeting:
- Plan your spending.
- Stick to the plan no matter what.

Budgeting is telling your money where you want it to go rather than wondering where it went.

We know that:

- Few people would consider driving their cars without a fuel gauge because they know the dangers and inconvenience of running out of fuel.
- Most people operate their personal finances without a spending gauge.
- Some people casually and impulsively spend from day to day and when they run out of money by the middle of the month they say, "Oops! I'm out of money. Now what do I do?"

Three: Solomon advises us to save for the future

The Principle of Saving

Go to the ant, you sluggard; consider its ways and be wise. It has no commander, no overseer or ruler, yet it stores its provisions in summer and gathers its food at harvest. Proverbs 6:6-8

Solomon reminds us that even bugs are smart enough to save. They do not consume all their resources immediately. They save some, storing it away for the future. But we are part of a "Live for today" culture. We want it all and we want it now. It is hard for us to save. Apparently, a high percentage of people end up with little in cash savings when they reach retirement. During their working years they had a reasonable income but at retirement they have little to show for it because for all their working years, they "paid" little if anything into a savings account. So, how much should we save?

Most financial experts recommend that we should put at least the equivalent of three months of our earnings in a savings account for unforeseen events such as sickness or redundancy. Thereafter, much will depend on your personal circumstances but many experts consider that at least 10% of your income should be saved for the future and it would be wise to save even more. But however the sum that you need to save for your future is calculated, you must get into the habit of saving some of your income. It really is one of those times when "the sooner the better" is the best advice I can give you and I know Solomon would agree with me.

While people understand the need to spend less now and save for the future, many will not. They would rather buy lottery tickets than save and they are foolish because paying into the lottery fund does not represent good value for your money. You are more likely to be hit by a meteor or go to the moon than you are to win the lottery. There is a simple word for the majority of people who play the lottery. It is the word "loser" and there are millions of them every week! Those who run the lottery count on "losers" and continually advertise for more of them. It is as foolish to waste money on things like the lottery as it is to waste money buying impulsively or on goods that you do not need.

The Bible teaches that we should save for the future but, as I have mentioned, many of us will not do so. We are not committed to the principle of delayed satisfaction. We refuse to endure the hardship of saving now for a future pay off.

Many, especially the young, shop with total disregard to their financial position. They yield to the temptation to use credit cards or loans for things that they want to enjoy now. Then, when unexpected problems and expenses occur, because they have not saved for the future, they are forced to borrow from the future and to pay high interest charges for the privilege. That is how loans and credit cards work. You commit your income for years ahead so that you can buy now. You hope that all will go well for you in the future because if it does not, you will still have the debts yet only a limited income to pay them off. You will be tempted to borrow again and so begins the downward spiral of debt that it is so difficult to escape from.

Using a credit card is so easy but statistics show that when we shop with plastic we spend 23% more than when we use cash. The experts say that when we use a credit card, it does not feel as though we are spending real money. It only feels very real when the bill comes!

In the adverts for loans and credit cards, you will read beautifully worded statements like, "Get the freedom to buy what you want when you want it!" But what they are really offering you is the ability to pay for something you cannot afford and a debt. The repayments will soon make you realise that in the "Get the freedom to buy what you want when you want it," statement, the word "debt" does not appear. That is what you now have but the word "debt" is an uncomfortable, unpleasant word as many only discover when the statements and the demands arrive.

Four: Solomon advises us to be content

The Principle of Modest Living

"Indulging in luxuries, wine and rich food, will never make you wealthy..." Proverbs 21:17

"It is better to be satisfied—content—with what you have than to always be wanting something else." Ecclesiastes 6:9

The problem is that so many of us are not content. Our yearnings exceed our earnings. And this is sad because earnings in the United Kingdom exceed those of the vast majority of the people on this planet. If you own a car, you are in the top 6% of the world's population and if you own a house you are in the top 3%. But so often we are not content with what we have and we want a better house, a newer car and more clothes. We see things we want but cannot afford. We buy them anyway believing the salesman who tells us that we can own this or that by paying easy monthly payments. I do not know about you but I have never known an easy monthly payment. They are all hard! We overspend until we have nightmares wondering how we are going to pay our bills.

Maybe we should live by the philosophy that says:

"Use it up, wear it out, make it do or do without!"

I like that! We would all be happier if we were content to live by that philosophy!

Five: Solomon advises us to give to God

The Principle of Tithing

"Honour the Lord with your wealth and with the best part of everything your land produces." Proverbs 3:9-10

Why tithe? Why give at least a tenth back to God. Let me give you four reasons. Tithing is an act:

- Of obedience.
- Of gratitude.
- That indicates priority.
- Of faith.

First: Tithing is an Act of Obedience

We should tithe as an act of obedience because the Bible clearly and repeatedly suggests giving a minimum of 10% back to God. For example in Malachi God says:

"Bring the whole tithe into the storehouse, that there may be food in my house." Malachi 3:10

Second: Tithing is an Act of Gratitude

Tithing is also an act of gratitude. When we give the first tenth we are saying to God that we would not have anything if it was not for Him and we thank Him. For as His Word says:

"Every good and perfect gift is from above coming down from the Father of the heavenly lights who does not change like shifting shadows." James 1:17

Third: Tithing is an Act that Indicates Priority

It is a way of saying, "God, I want You to be number one in my life and I prove it by putting You first in my money."

Fourth: Tithing is an Act of Faith

It is a way of saying, "God, I know that all those promises in the Bible say that if I put You first you will take care of me. To prove that I believe these promises I am going to give to you first." And God takes care of us like no one else as David said in the 23rd Psalm:

"...my cup overflows." Psalm 23:5

In the verse from Malachi 3 God goes on to say:

"Test Me in this, and see if I will not throw open the floodgates of heaven and pour out so much blessing that you will not have room enough for it." Malachi 3:10

And Solomon says that if we give to God from the best:

"He will fill your barns with grain, and your vats will overflow with the finest wine." Proverbs 3:10

In these verses and others like them, the call to tithe is accompanied by a promise that God will intervene supernaturally in the financial affairs of those who consistently tithe. They will enjoy financial miracles that would not happen if they neglected to give to God. Our giving to God should not be viewed as a debt we owe but as a seed we sow, a seed that will yield God's bountiful blessings.

By the way, Malachi 3 verse 10 is the only verse in the Bible that says you can prove God. In essence our Heavenly Father says, "You want to prove that I exist? Start tithing. Then watch what happens!" It may not make sense but I can tell you by experience that it works. When we trust God by giving our tithe to Him, He responds by taking care of us. I can say that I have never even missed what I have given for I have found God to be completely trustworthy. And when you think about it, we do not have trouble trusting God with other things. We trust Him with our eternal destiny. We trust Him for daily wisdom and guidance. Why cannot we trust Him with our money!?

People ask, "Should I tithe the net or the gross?" and my reply is "Well, that depends. What do you want God to bless, your net or your gross?

God blesses most the areas of our lives where we have put Him first. If you truly put Him first in your marriage, it is going to be absolutely wonderful. If you put Him first in your career, He will help you make a difference in this world that others will notice. If you doubt me, then read the Old Testament stories of the lives of Joseph and Daniel. If you put God first in your parenting, it will help with your children.

If we handle our money in the 'Solomon way' we will not just be free from stress, we will also experience another blessing. We will be able to join God in His work by putting ourselves in a position to help others. We will have the financial ability to come to the aid of people who need it. Habits of saving and careful spending will make it possible for us to use our excess funds to minister to others. We will be free to respond to the Holy Spirit's prompting to finance a big project or give a big gift. There is nothing more frustrating than having your heart pound with the passion to offer your resources for God's use but be in such financial bondage that you cannot and this is sad because there are few things in life that bring us more fun than doing exactly that! In 1 Timothy Paul says that generous giving to help others makes it possible for us to:

"...take hold of the life that is truly life!" 1Timothy 6:19

Many of you have been able to experience this special joy over the years. You have given to help people physically, emotionally and spiritually. Would it feel good to know that your money, your wealth, was such that you could do something like that again? Giving for a godly cause leaves a feeling that will go on and on. It will not fade like the joy we get at buying a new car, a TV or an outfit. I challenge you to follow these guidelines in Proverbs and manage your money so you can do things like this.

If you have not done so already, give God control of your finances. Do not just invite Him into your heart. Invite Him into your cheque book. Ask Him to guide you when it comes to how you handle your money.

Chapter 12

How To Make The Most Of Your Life

We all know that age is relative. One lady said that her five-year-old granddaughter asked her, "Grandma, were you on the ark with Noah?" She said, "Of course not!" Her granddaughter replied, "Well, why didn't you drown?" When you are five, eighteen sounds old and at eighteen, forty sounds old. When you are forty, seventy sounds old and at seventy, ninety sounds old. When you are ninety nothing sounds old!

We tend to divide life into stages. In his play, "As You Like It," Shakespeare wrote that there are seven stages of life because he observed that:

"All the world's a stage
And all the men and women merely players,

They have their exits and entrances,
And one man in his time plays many parts,
His acts being seven ages.
At first the infant, mewling and puking in the nurse's arms.
Then, the whining schoolboy with his satchel
And shining morning face, creeping like a snail
Unwillingly to school.
And then the lover,
Sighing like a furnace, with a woeful ballad..."

In stages four and five the lover becomes a soldier and then a judge. Stage six is old age and Shakespeare concludes:

"Last scene of all,
That ends this strange eventful history,
Is second childishness and mere oblivion,
Sans teeth, sans eyes, sans taste, sans everything."

I think the ancients understood the stages of life better than Shakespeare did and certainly better than we do. The Aberdeen Bestiary is a collection of 11th Century writings from the North of England. These allegorical stories about animals are purported to have come from an ancient Greek writer. There is a fascinating section which describes the six stages of a person's life and I like these age divisions better than the ones we use today:

Infancy: Birth to age 7 years

Childhood: 8 to 14 years
Adolescence: 14 to 28 years
Youth: 29 to 50 years
Maturity: 51 – 69 years
Riper years: 70 onwards

Some of these age divisions are radical. I like the expression "riper years" and I guess quite a few of us like the "youth" classification. "Adolescence" fits in well with the fact that so many young adults are still having problems!

Whether you are tiny or ninety and regardless of which description or classification of yourself you personally prefer, the Bible says how we should live our lives.

Peter addressed this important subject in his first letter:

"Therefore, since Christ suffered in his body, arm yourselves also with the same attitude, because he who has suffered in his body is done with sin." 1Peter 4:1

"The end of all things is near. Therefore be clear minded and self-controlled so that you can pray. Above all, love each other deeply, because love covers over a multitude of sins. Offer hospitality to one another without grumbling. Each one should use whatever gift he has received to serve others, faithfully administering God's grace in its various forms. If anyone speaks, he should do it as one speaking the very words of God. If anyone serves, he should do it with the strength God provides, so that in all things God may be praised through Jesus Christ. To him be the glory and the power for ever and ever. Amen. Dear friends, do not be surprised at the painful trial you are suffering, as though something strange were happening to you." 1Peter 4:7-11

Peter picks out three important directives that we must understand and obey. They are:

- Pray.
- Love.
- Serve.

If you follow God's directions in these areas, the rest of your life really can be the best of your life!

FIRST: Pray with a sense of urgency

"The end of all things is near. Therefore be clear minded and self-controlled so that you can pray." 1Peter 4:7

Have you ever watched a football team when they are playing in extra time? They perform at a higher level. Time is short and they must take advantage of the time that they have left. That is what we should be doing because Peter says the end is near. So let us start praying as if we are in extra time.

When you read the New Testament that was written in the first century, it is clear that the early Christians expected Jesus to return in their lifetimes. Some two thousand years have passed and Jesus has not yet returned. Did those early Christians get it wrong? No, because Jesus taught His disciples to expect Him at any time. He wanted His own, those He was coming back from Heaven for, to live their lives ready and prepared for His return whenever it happened.

In Mark Chapter 13 Jesus spoke about the time of His return. He said:

"The exact day and hour? No one knows that, not even heaven's angels, not even the Son. Only the Father. So keep a sharp lookout, for you do not know the timetable. It is like a man who takes a trip, leaving home and putting his servants in charge, each assigned a task, and commanding the gatekeeper to stand watch. So stay at your post, watching. You have no idea when the homeowner is returning. You do not want him showing up unannounced, with you asleep on the job." Mark 13:32-36. The Message

These words of Jesus are on the last page of the Bible:

"I am coming soon." Revelation 22:20

Jesus did not say when but He did confirm that He was coming soon. So you see why we need to pray with a sense of urgency

The great missionary to China, Hudson Taylor wrote:

"I have seen many men work without praying, though I have never seen any good come out of it; but I have never seen a man pray without working."

Since the return of Jesus is closer than ever, we must not work and pray as though we have unlimited time to tell people about Jesus. Millions are dying every day without Him and when He returns the opportunity to spread the good news will end. We need to pray:

- For God to send labourers into the harvest.
- That God will save people who do not know Him.
- For boldness so we can share the gospel across the street and across the globe.

SECOND: Love by showing hospitality

"Above all, love each other deeply, because love covers over a multitude of sins. Offer hospitality to one another without grumbling."1Peter 4:8-9

Love is the most important directive we can follow. Jesus said that all the Old Testament Commandments could be summarised in just two:

- First: Love God with all your being.
- Second: Love your neighbour as yourself.

Peter gives us two important qualities of love:

- The First Quality of Love: Love covers sins.
- The Second Quality of Love: Love is hospitable.

The First Quality of Love: Love covers sins

Peter states:

"...love covers a multitude of sins." 1Peter 4:8

This does not mean that when I love it covers my sins. It means that the best kind of love covers the sins of those we love. In Proverbs we also read that:

"Love covers all wrongs." Proverbs 10:12

The language used in First Peter and Proverbs of "covering sin" refers to an incident that happened back in Genesis 9 where we read the story of Noah. Noah was a righteous man who obeyed God and built a large boat because a flood was coming. Because of his faith and obedience Noah and his family were saved from the flood. Do you know what happened to Noah after the flood? You do not hear this part of the story in Sunday School but it is in the Bible. It is a lesson to everyone that nobody except Jesus is perfect.

Noah planted a vineyard and got into the wine making business. He sampled his own wine and got so drunk that he undressed and was naked. His adult sons could have laughed at him and embarrassed him but because they loved him, two of them got a cloak. They walked backwards so that they would not see their father's nakedness and they placed the cloak over him to cover him. Why did they show such concern for their drunken father? They loved him. That is what the Bible means when it says in First Corinthians that:

"...love keeps no record of wrongs." 1Corinthians 13:5

Is there somebody who needs your love? Do not even think about considering what they have done wrong or whether they are worth it or not. Why? Because when you love somebody, as Noah's sons loved him, you cover what they have done wrong, whatever that wrong is and whether they are worth it or not. Who do you know that needs that kind of covering love from you?

We all need God's covering love. God could look at us and see all the filth and dirt of our sin but instead He says to us, "I have covered you. Your sins are covered forever." We know that because Paul wrote:

"God demonstrates his own love for us in this: While we were still sinners, Christ died for us." Romans 5:8

The Second Quality of Love: Love is hospitable

Peter's second quality of love concerns:

"...hospitality" 1Peter 4:9

One of the most visible expressions of love is hospitality. Entertaining is not hospitality so do not confuse them:

- Entertaining is having friends in your home, those you know you will enjoy.
  Hospitality is having strangers in your home.
- Entertaining is a social grace that will give something back to you.

Hospitality is an expression of love that never seeks reward or recognition.

- Entertaining focuses on the host or their beautiful home or cooking skills.
Hospitality focuses on the needs of the guest.

Hospitality goes against our self-centred nature:

- Hospitality is neglected because we feel much more comfortable hiding away with our families and friends in our castles.

Our self-centredness is like gravity:

Gravity keeps us on the ground and stops us from flying into space.
Like gravity, our selfish nature wants to withdraw within ourselves and within our homes.

However powerful gravity is, we overcome it whenever we fly. It requires thrust from an aeroplane's engines and lift from its wings but gravity can be overcome.

Hospitality also takes a lot of effort but when we are hospitable to strangers, we overcome selfishness. It is neither natural nor easy. That is why Peter asks us to:

"...show hospitality without grumbling." 1Peter 4:9

Have you broken free from the bonds of self-centredness and discovered the exhilaration of soaring love expressed as hospitality? Let me ask you two questions to help you consider and understand the point that Peter is making:

- Who are the people you have had as guests in your home over the past six months?
- Is your answer, "only family and friends?"

The "only family and friends" answer means that you only entertain and are not hospitable. One of the best ways to show the love of Jesus is to make friends with strangers by showing them hospitality.

In Genesis 18 we read about Abraham showing hospitality to three strangers who approached his tent. They looked like ordinary men but two of them were angels. Abraham did not realise who they were until later but he welcomed them, washed their feet and fed them. What a lesson! If you never open your home to strangers, you may miss an opportunity to meet angels. We read in Hebrews:

"Do not forget to entertain strangers...some people have entertained angels without knowing it." Hebrews 13:2

If you want the rest of your life to be the best of your life, try hospitality:

- Look for opportunities to have strangers in your home.

- Give them a meal and give them the love of Jesus.

THIRD: Serve with a spirit of authority

"Each one should use whatever gift he has received to serve others, faithfully administering God's grace in its various forms." 1Peter 4:10

You were not saved to sit, you were saved to serve! And God has given you at least one spiritual gift to serve with. This special gift will enable you to serve God by serving others. It is not a natural ability, it is a supernatural ability. You will not enjoy the rest of your life very much unless you find out what your spiritual gifts are and start using them. Too many Christians are sitting in the pews using one excuse or another for doing nothing.

There is a quote from an unknown source which I like.

"If you are not involved in any service, what excuse have you used?

Abraham was old
Jacob was insecure
Joseph was abused
Moses stuttered
Samson was co-dependent
Rahab was immoral
David had an affair and all kinds of family problems
Elijah was suicidal

Jeremiah was depressed
Jonah was reluctant
Naomi was a widow
Peter was impulsive and hot-tempered
Martha worried a lot
Thomas had doubts
Paul had poor health
Timothy was timid.

That list discloses quite a variety of people but God used each of them in His service and if you will stop making excuses, He will use you too.

Depending on how you count them, there are fourteen to eighteen different spiritual gifts mentioned in the New Testament. We discover in First Peter that spiritual gifts fall into two broad categories. They are the:

- Speaking gifts
- Service gifts

First: The Speaking Gifts

Some of you have the ability to teach or preach and some are very good at encouraging others. Some of you feel inadequate because you do not feel very comfortable speaking whether publicly or to small groups. That presents no problem because you may have the ability to help clean the church building, visit hospitals or set out chairs and tables for the various church activities. Yes, they are vital gifts too. Whatever your gift is, you need to use it with God's authority. If your gift is teaching or preaching, Peter says:

"...let it be God's words" 1Peter 4:11. The Message

The Old Testament prophets spoke with God's authority. They said, "Thus says the Lord!" We do the same when we say, "The Bible says..."

Because the Bible is the inspired Word of God, you are not reading my message for you. You are reading God's message for you personally at this moment.

Second: The Serving Gifts

If your gift is serving, these words of guidance must be at the forefront of your thoughts and strategy:

- Serving God can be physically draining.
- In your own strength you will fail.
- God's strength is available to you.
- What you do in God's strength will succeed.
- Learn to depend entirely on God's strength.

The great Bible teacher, Donald Grey Barnhouse, wrote about an American citizen who was arrested during a Latin-American revolution. He was sentenced to death by firing squad simply for being an American. The American Ambassador was outraged. He wrapped an American flag around his own body and stood between the condemned American and the firing squad. He said, "If you shoot this man, you will have to shoot through this flag. If you shoot this flag you will incur the wrath of the entire American Nation." It worked. The American was released. In the same way, we are Ambassadors for Christ and we are wrapped in His righteousness. Wherever you serve God and whatever you do, remember that you have the authority of heaven itself!

One of Christianity's great men was Hudson Taylor. One day in 1849, when he was 17, although he had no interest in spiritual matters, he was so bored that he read a Christian booklet that referred to the millions of Chinese who had never heard about Jesus. That day God broke his heart and from that moment, his passion was to share the love of God with the Chinese people.

At 21 he travelled to China and began preaching the gospel but his first years were frustrating because few people responded. A wise Chinese man pointed out that his English suit had extra buttons on the sleeves and backs but there were no button holes and he asked why. He realised that his English suits were distracting his listeners. From that point he learnt to speak Mandarin and he dressed in the Chinese custom. He discovered God did not want the Chinese to become English Christians but to become Chinese Christians.

He later returned to England where he translated the New Testament into Chinese and convinced others to join him in China. He returned with several other missionaries. He faced many hardships including the death of his wife and child but God gave him the strength to maintain his work. In one city, a middle-aged man was one of the leaders of a reformed Buddhist group. He had long sought for the truth by studying Buddhism, Taoism, and the writings of Confucius. When Hudson Taylor shared the good news of Jesus with him, the man found the peace and truth for which he had been searching. He became a Christian and started preaching to his fellow Chinese. Shortly after his conversion, he asked Hudson Taylor for how long the message of Jesus had been known in England. When he was told that it had been known for hundreds of years the man was shocked. He said, "What? For hundreds of years you have had these glad tidings and only now have come to teach it to us? My father sought after the truth for more than twenty years and died without finding it. Oh, why did you not come sooner?"

Hudson Taylor was a small shy man and physically weak but because he trusted God many today consider him to be a spiritual giant. He devoted fifty years of his life to sharing the love of God with the Chinese. He died in 1905. As a result of his work, over two hundred and fifty mission stations had been established and over one hundred thousand Chinese had become Christians.

The secret of Hudson Taylor's effectiveness was that he had learnt to depend upon God's strength instead of his own. If you want to experience true fulfilment, you must learn the same secret. He wrote:

"I ... am not especially gifted, and am shy by nature, but my gracious and merciful God and Father inclined Himself to me, and when I was weak in faith He strengthened me while I was still young. He taught me in my helplessness to rest on Him, and to pray even about little things in which another might have felt able to help himself."

He.... went through three stages of understanding the secret of God's strength. He said that:
"I used to ask God if He would come and help me...and then I asked God if I might come and help Him...and then I ended by asking God to do His work through me."

Have you made the same discovery as Hudson Taylor? When you have, the best of your life can be the rest of your life. Here is how:

- Pray like never before because God's clock is winding down.
- Love others so deeply that you welcome strangers into your life.
- Give your life to others but do it in God's strength.

Copyright Notices

Other books by Derek Stringer include:

Moving Up To The Next Level
Facing A New Day
Reigning In Life
Lessons From A Rainbow
Over Conquer
Great Bible Questions

Dr. Stringer travels internationally preaching at Churches, Bible Conferences and Bible Schools.

Good News Broadcasting Association (GB)
Ranskill DN22 8NN United Kingdom
Email: info@gnba.net Internet: www.gnba.net

Good News Broadcasting Association (GB)

TEACHING THE WORD AND TOUCHING THE WORLD

Sounding Out . . .

A free bi-monthly news letter with news of our radio ministry internationally, a devotional message and resources for living the Christian life.

Free Email Messages

Derek also writes a devotional Bible message for the fortnightly GNB Email News, which has a wide international readership. To be added to the mailing list contact news@gnba.net

GNB CD . . .

A bi-monthly magazine style Bible teaching CD giving approximately 75 minutes of varied ministry including Derek Stringer. A very popular resource.

More details of the above and how you can become a Ministry Partner are available from:

Good News Broadcasting Association (GB)
Ranskill DN22 8NN United Kingdom
Email: info@gnba.net Internet: www.gnba.net